CAITRÍONA DALY

Caitríona Daly is a playwright and screenwriter from Dublin. She was the eighth recipient of the Irish Theatre Institute's Phelim Donlon Bursary and Residency Award. She has also received Writers' Guild of Ireland Awards for Best Theatre Script for her play *Duck Duck Goose* which was produced by Fishamble: The New Play Company in 2021; and for Best Continuing Drama Script for her work on the BBC Drama *Doctors* in 2024. Her plays *Test Dummy* and *Normal* have previously been nominated for an Irish Times Theatre Award for Best New Play and The Fishamble New Writing Prize, respectively. Her work has been translated and produced internationally. When not writing, she teaches creative writing, script writing and drama all over Ireland.

Other Titles in this Series

Chris Bush
THE ASSASSINATION OF KATIE HOPKINS
  with Matt Winkworth
THE CHANGING ROOM
CHRIS BUSH PLAYS: ONE
A DOLL'S HOUSE *after* Ibsen
FAUSTUS: THAT DAMNED WOMAN
HUNGRY
JANE EYRE *after* Brontë
THE LAST NOËL
OTHERLAND
ROBIN HOOD AND THE
  CHRISTMAS HEIST
  with Matt Winkworth
ROCK / PAPER / SCISSORS
STANDING AT THE SKY'S EDGE
  with Richard Hawley
STEEL

Jez Butterworth
THE FERRYMAN
THE HILLS OF CALIFORNIA
JERUSALEM
JEZ BUTTERWORTH PLAYS: ONE
JEZ BUTTERWORTH PLAYS: TWO
MOJO
THE NIGHT HERON
PARLOUR SONG
THE RIVER
THE WINTERLING

Caryl Churchill
BLUE HEART
CHURCHILL PLAYS: THREE
CHURCHILL PLAYS: FOUR
CHURCHILL PLAYS: FIVE
CHURCHILL: SHORTS
CLOUD NINE
DING DONG THE WICKED
A DREAM PLAY *after* Strindberg
DRUNK ENOUGH TO SAY I LOVE YOU?
ESCAPED ALONE
FAR AWAY
GLASS. KILL. BLUEBEARD'S FRIENDS. IMP.
HERE WE GO
HOTEL
ICECREAM
LIGHT SHINING IN BUCKINGHAMSHIRE
LOVE AND INFORMATION
MAD FOREST
A NUMBER
PIGS AND DOGS
SEVEN JEWISH CHILDREN
THE SKRIKER
THIS IS A CHAIR
THYESTES *after* Seneca
TRAPS
WHAT IF IF ONLY

Caitríona Daly
DUCK DUCK GOOSE

Nancy Harris
THE BEACON
NO ROMANCE
OUR NEW GIRL
THE RED SHOES
SOMEWHERE OUT THERE YOU
TWO LADIES

Deirdre Kinahan
CROSSINGS
DEIRDRE KINAHAN: SHORTS
HALCYON DAYS
MOMENT
RAGING: THREE PLAYS/SEVEN YEARS
  OF WARFARE IN IRELAND
RATHMINES ROAD
THE SAVIOUR
SPINNING
THE UNMANAGEABLE SISTERS
  after Michel Tremblay

Lucy Kirkwood
BEAUTY AND THE BEAST
  with Katie Mitchell
BLOODY WIMMIN
THE CHILDREN
CHIMERICA
HEDDA *after* Ibsen
THE HUMAN BODY
IT FELT EMPTY WHEN THE HEART
  WENT AT FIRST BUT IT IS
  ALRIGHT NOW
LUCY KIRKWOOD PLAYS: ONE
MOSQUITOES
NSFW
RAPTURE
TINDERBOX
THE WELKIN

Shaan Sahota
THE ESTATE

Jack Thorne
2ND MAY 1997
AFTER LIFE *after* Hirokazu Kore-eda
BUNNY
BURYING YOUR BROTHER IN
  THE PAVEMENT
A CHRISTMAS CAROL *after* Dickens
THE END OF HISTORY…
HOPE
JACK THORNE PLAYS: ONE
JACK THORNE PLAYS: TWO
JUNKYARD
LET THE RIGHT ONE IN
  after John Ajvide Lindqvist
THE MOTIVE AND THE CUE
MYDIDAE
THE SOLID LIFE OF SUGAR WATER
STACY & FANNY AND FAGGOT
WHEN WINSTON WENT TO WAR WITH
  THE WIRELESS
WHEN YOU CURE ME
WOYZECK *after* Büchner

debbie tucker green
BORN BAD
DEBBIE TUCKER GREEN PLAYS: ONE
DIRTY BUTTERFLY
EAR FOR EYE
HANG
NUT
A PROFOUNDLY AFFECTIONATE,
  PASSIONATE DEVOTION TO
  SOMEONE (– *NOUN*)
RANDOM
STONING MARY
TRADE & GENERATIONS
TRUTH AND RECONCILIATION

Caitríona Daly

THE LUNCH PUNCH POWER HOUR IN CONFERENCE ROOM 4

NICK HERN BOOKS
London
www.nickhernbooks.co.uk

A Nick Hern Book

The Lunch Punch Power Hour in Conference Room 4 first published in Great Britain in 2025 as a paperback original by Nick Hern Books Limited, The Glasshouse, 49a Goldhawk Road, London W12 8QP, in association with the Abbey Theatre, Dublin

The Lunch Punch Power Hour in Conference Room 4 copyright © 2025 Caitríona Daly

Caitríona Daly has asserted her right to be identified as the author of this work

Front cover: photography by Ros Kavanagh

Designed and typeset by Nick Hern Books, London
Printed in Great Britain by Mimeo Ltd, Huntingdon, Cambridgeshire PE29 6XX

A CIP catalogue record for this book is available from the British Library

ISBN 978 1 83904 494 6

CAUTION All rights whatsoever in this play are strictly reserved. Requests to reproduce the text in whole or in part should be addressed to the publisher. This book may not be used, in whole or in part, for the development or training of artificial intelligence technologies or systems.

Amateur Performing Rights Applications for performance, including readings and excerpts, by amateurs in the English language throughout the world should be addressed to the Performing Rights Manager, Nick Hern Books, The Glasshouse, 49a Goldhawk Road, London W12 8QP, *tel* +44 (0)20 8749 4953, *email* rights@nickhernbooks.co.uk, except as follows:

Australia: ORiGiN Theatrical, *email* enquiries@originmusic.com.au, *web* www.origintheatrical.com.au

New Zealand: Play Bureau, 20 Rua Street, Mangapapa, Gisborne, 4010, *tel* +64 21 258 3998, *email* info@playbureau.com

Professional Performing Rights Applications for performance by professionals in any medium and in any language throughout the world should be addressed to Sovran Carey Ltd, Spade Centre, St Paul's, North King Street, Dublin 7, D07 CX22, Ireland, *email* rights@sovrancarey.com

No performance of any kind may be given unless a licence has been obtained. Applications should be made before rehearsals begin. Publication of this play does not necessarily indicate its availability for amateur performance.

www.nickhernbooks.co.uk/environmental-policy

Nick Hern Books' authorised representative in the EU is
Easy Access System Europe – Mustamäe tee 50, 10621 Tallinn, Estonia
email gpsr.requests@easproject.com

World Premiere
An Abbey Theatre production

The Lunch Punch Power Hour in Conference Room 4
By Caitríona Daly

An Abbey Theatre commission

First performed on 31 July 2025 at the Abbey Theatre, Dublin

CAST

The Receptionist Formerly Known as Jess	Emma Dargan-Reid
Daniel	Fionn Foley
HR Lady Susan	Helen Norton
Clodagh	Caoimhe O'Malley
Crónán / Frank	Bryan Quinn

CREATIVES

Playwright	Caitríona Daly
Director	Raymond Keane
Set Design	Ronán Duffy
Costume Design	Saileóg O'Halloran
Lighting Design	Dara Hoban
Composition and Sound Design	Jenny O'Malley
Dramaturg	Ruth McGowan
Voice Director	Andrea Ainsworth
Hair and Make-Up	Leonard Daly
Fight Director	Alan Walsh
Casting Director	Barry Coyle

COMPANY

Producer	Jen Coppinger
Production Manager	Andy Keogh
Production Coordinator	Justin Murphy
Assistant Producer	Aoife McCollum
Company Manager	Danny Erskine
Company Stage Manager	Clive Welsh
Deputy Stage Manager	Leanne Vaughey
Assistant Stage Manager	Anika Kidd
Costume Supervisor	Síofra Ní Chiardha
Props Master	Eimer Murphy
Props Supervisor	Dyan Farrell
Publicity	Mia O'Reilly
Marketing	Heather Maher
Social Media	Eva Louise Ó Broin
Publicity Image	Ros Kavanagh
Access Co-Ordinator	Daragh McMahon
Audio Description	Mo Harte
Artistic Director/Co-Director	Caitríona McLaughlin
Executive Director/Co-Director	Mark O'Brien

THE ABBEY THEATRE

As Ireland's national theatre, the Abbey Theatre's ambition is to enrich the cultural lives of everyone with a curiosity for and interest in Irish theatre, stories, artists and culture. Courage and imagination are at the heart of our storytelling, while inclusivity, diversity and equality are at the core of our thinking. Led by Co-Directors Caitríona McLaughlin (Artistic Director) and Mark O'Brien (Executive Director), the Abbey Theatre celebrates both the rich canon of Irish dramatic writing and the potential of future generations of Irish theatre artists.

Ireland has a rich history of theatre and playwriting and extraordinary actors, designers and directors. Artists are at the heart of our organisation, with Marina Carr and Conor McPherson as Senior Associate Playwrights and Caroline Byrne as Associate Director.

Our stories teach us what it is to belong, what it is to be excluded and to exclude. Artistically our programme is built on twin impulses, and around two questions: 'who we were, and who are we now?' We interrogate our classical canon with an urgency about what makes it speak to this moment. On our stages we find and champion new voices and new ways of seeing, our purpose – to identify combinations of characters we are yet to meet, having conversations we are yet to hear.

ABBEY THEATRE SUPPORTERS

PROGRAMME PARTNER

CORPORATE GUARDIANS

Bloomberg   ESB
Irish Life   THE IRISH TIMES
NORTHERN TRUST

RETAIL PARTNER

ARNOTTS

GOLD AMBASSADORS

Ipsos B&A   ecclesiastical
McCann FitzGerald   FLYNN HODKINSON

HOSPITALITY PARTNER

THE WESTBURY
THE DOYLE COLLECTION · DUBLIN

IT PARTNER

Qualcom

SILVER AMBASSADOR

Interpath   ODGERS BERNDTSON
wines direct

RESTAURANT PARTNERS

DOLIER STREET   DUNNE & CRESCENZI
HAWKSMOOR   NANNETTI'S
CUCINA ITALIANA

GUARDIANS

The Cielinski Family
Deirdre and Irial Finan
Carmel and Martin Naughton
Sheelagh O'Neill
Donal Moore R.I.P.

VISIONARIES

Tony Ahearne
Pat and Kate Butler
Dr. Leisha Daly
Janice Flynn

INNOVATORS

Gerard and Liv McNaughton
Cecily O'Neill
Louise Richardson R.I.P.

CHAMPION

Tommy Gibbons
Eugene Magee
Andrew and Delyth Parkes

CREATORS

Cathy Allen
Frances Britton
Margaret Roohan
Charles Young

EXPLORERS

Valerie Cole
Thelma Doran
Peter Howlett
Mary and Kevin Hoy
John Gabriel Irwin
Anne Lardener
Janet O'Brien
Tina Robinson
Kathleen Walsh

We want to thank the listed supporters for their ongoing generosity and belief in Ireland's National Theatre. We would also like to thank our generous supporters who have asked to remain anonymous.

Characters

THE RECEPTIONIST FKA JESS, *late twenties, caustic but never fully confident in their own bite. Her background in academia means at times there is a childlike wonder and curiosity about her. Pronouns She or They.*

CLODAGH, *late thirties/early forties. Confident in what she knows, scared of what she doesn't. A sizeable ego with low self-esteem. Pronouns She/Her.*

DANIEL, *late thirties. A gormless but likeable man. Funnels most of his emotions in indirect methods. Probably the GAA. Pronouns He/Him.*

HR LADY SUSAN, *mid-forties. Getting through life with gritted teeth and a forced smile. Pronouns She/Her.*

CRÓNÁN (*voice-over*), *early forties. A self-proclaimed enigmatic leader who is not as smart as he thinks he is.*

FRANK (*voice-over*), *early fifties. A salt-of-the-earth working man. Should be played by the same actor who is playing Crónán.*

Setting

The Docklands, Dublin, Ireland, present day.

Note on Text

A forward slash (/) indicates when the following line is spoken.

Words in [square brackets] are unspoken.

Author's Note

The props, costumes and music mentioned in the script should be seen as suggestions for production rather than necessities.

This text went to press before the end of rehearsals and so may differ slightly from the play as performed.

A standard corporate boardroom. There is a door to a corridor in the back of the centre-stage that has a narrow floor-to-ceiling plexiglas window beside it. The door is ajar. There is a comically large boardroom table and several chairs. Cabinets border the room. Cups, mugs, glasses, a Nespresso machine and bottles of water line them.

Preset: THE RECEPTIONIST FKA JESS *sits at the top of the boardroom table eating their lunch. They have their feet on the table and are wearing a receptionist's headset around their neck and are probably reading a laborious-looking book.*

CLODAGH *arrives at the doorway wheeling a large briefcase with her. She stops and looks at* THE RECEPTIONIST FKA JESS *for a while.*

THE RECEPTIONIST FKA JESS *doesn't notice. They've just put a mouthful of tagine in their mouth when* CLODAGH *interrupts with a loud cough. The food almost comes out of their nose. They look around.*

THE RECEPTIONIST FKA JESS (*coughing*). Oh, sorry.

    THE RECEPTIONIST FKA JESS *takes their feet off the table.*

CLODAGH. You're not allowed eat your lunch in here.

THE RECEPTIONIST FKA JESS. Yeah, I know. I just reckoned, there's nothing booked in here until after two so –

    CLODAGH *wheels her briefcase behind her and walks into the room.*

CLODAGH. There *is* something booked in here, actually.

THE RECEPTIONIST FKA JESS. Oh… it's not in the diary.

CLODAGH. Not in whose diary? It's in my diary.

...IN CONFERENCE ROOM 4   11

THE RECEPTIONIST FKA JESS. I mean, the room's diary.

CLODAGH. The room has a diary?

THE RECEPTIONIST FKA JESS.... Yes?

THE RECEPTIONIST FKA JESS waits for CLODAGH to respond. Until the silence becomes evident that she's not going to.

I'm sure there was probably an oversight.

CLODAGH. Yes. Obviously. There's a lunchroom on the third floor, you know. If the kitchenette is too much of a bother for you?

THE RECEPTIONIST FKA JESS. It's too... distracting. I like to read.

CLODAGH gives her a look like La-Di-Da and then waits for her to leave.

THE RECEPTIONIST FKA JESS gets up from their seat, gathers their belongings and heads for the door.

CLODAGH. Please clean up before you leave.

THE RECEPTIONIST FKA JESS looks around the room blankly. Clean what?

THE RECEPTIONIST FKA JESS takes their sleeve and begins to wipe where their bowl and feet has been.

CLODAGH sighs.

THE RECEPTIONIST FKA JESS leaves.

CLODAGH wheels her oversized briefcase to the right-hand side of the table.

She sits down, deep in thought.

She sees an electric swatter across the room and moves for it determinedly.

She picks up and smiles maniacally. She begins to swipe it around as if she is fencing with it. She does it all with gusto.

DANIEL walks into the room with another large wheelie briefcase. He pays very little attention to CLODAGH's fencing match. He places his briefcase on the other side of the table to CLODAGH's and leaves the room.

CLODAGH stops when she realises she's not alone any more and puts the swatter back.

DANIEL re-enters carrying a large bowl of soup.

They both stop when they see each other.

DANIEL. Hi Clodagh.

CLODAGH looks at him intensely and sits down. DANIEL follows.

CLODAGH takes a plastic box of kale salad and a plastic fork from her briefcase.

She smiles at DANIEL, insincerely, and begins to eat.

CLODAGH crunches on her kale aggressively at DANIEL. Unsure of what's going on, DANIEL begins to slurp his soup in retaliation.

The slurped soup and the crunched kale noises start a conversation with each other.

Sometimes it's a race, other times it's an elaborate beat or musical number until eventually the slurping and the crunching are almost fucking each other. They are about to reach a climax when a pathetic cough is heard at the doorway, where HR LADY SUSAN stands.

HR LADY SUSAN (*so saccharine it's sadistic*). Room for one more?

CLODAGH (*almost matching her sincerity*). Always for you, Susan.

DANIEL (*mouth full*). Hi Susan.

HR LADY SUSAN walks in and looks at their lunches, smiling.

HR LADY SUSAN. What has you in here today then?

CLODAGH. A lunchtime meeting.

HR LADY SUSAN. Oh right... What for? I didn't see it in the diary.

DANIEL. CSR surplus meeting.

CLODAGH. It's been okayed by Crónán.

HR LADY SUSAN (*smiling and laughing*). Still needs to be in the diary though.

CLODAGH (*smiling and laughing*). Well why don't you put it in the diary then?

HR LADY SUSAN (*smiling and laughing*). Too late to put it in now. Could be something else in the diary.

CLODAGH (*smiling and laughing*). There isn't anything else in the diary though?

HR LADY SUSAN (*smiling and laughing*). How would you know?

CLODAGH (*smiling and laughing*). The Receptionist told me, so.

HR LADY SUSAN (*smiling and laughing*). Wasn't that very good of her?

CLODAGH (*smiling and laughing*). Absolutely.

HR LADY SUSAN (*smiling and laughing*). Well the least you can do is put the food away anyway. Might cause a smell.

CLODAGH (*smiling and laughing*). It's kale, Susan. All it smells of is failure.

CLODAGH *and* HR LADY SUSAN *laugh in a hysterical but barbed manner and then stop abruptly.*

The intercom starts buzzing in the hall.

HR LADY SUSAN (*still smiling*). Put it away, Clodagh.

CLODAGH *and* DANIEL *put their spoon and fork down.*

HR LADY SUSAN *smiles and begins to walk around the room thinking.*

(*To herself.*) You're having a meeting…

CLODAGH. Yes.

HR LADY SUSAN. Yes.

Beat.

You've no quorum?

CLODAGH. Gareth is coming.

The intercom is still buzzing from the hall.

HR LADY SUSAN (*gleefully*). Gareth's not here today. He's having a colonoscopy.

CLODAGH *and* DANIEL. FUCKING GARETH.

HR LADY SUSAN. Now, now. We don't use that kind of language in the office now, do we?

The intercom keeps buzzing.

CLODAGH. Sorry, Susan.

DANIEL. Sorry.

CLODAGH. We can get a quorum.

DANIEL. Absolutely.

HR LADY SUSAN *grimaces in pain.*

The intercom keeps buzzing.

HR LADY SUSAN. Well no meeting without a quorum and no shenanigans either way, not like the last time. You were warned. And it's not the kind of behaviour we would like to see from a future Assistant Vice-President. Isn't that right, Clodagh?

CLODAGH*'s mask drops. She glares at* HR LADY SUSAN.

CLODAGH. Are you going to get the intercom, Susan?

HR LADY SUSAN. Yes, I am.

HR LADY SUSAN *stays standing, smiling aggressively back at* CLODAGH.

The intercom goes again, uninterrupted.

HR LADY SUSAN *runs to answer the intercom.*

CLODAGH *waits a beat and then runs out of the conference-room door. We see her run up and down the corridor, looking for anyone to join the meeting.*

CLODAGH *arrives, dragging* THE RECEPTIONIST FKA JESS *and their lunch with her.*

CLODAGH (*out of breath*). Now. There we are.

THE RECEPTIONIST FKA JESS *recovers from the whiplash.*

THE RECEPTIONIST FKA JESS. I thought we couldn't eat in here.

CLODAGH. Well would you prefer I returned you to the bathroom cubicle I found you in?

Beat.

THE RECEPTIONIST FKA JESS. No.

CLODAGH. Okay, then.

THE RECEPTIONIST FKA JESS. But you said we can't eat in here.

CLODAGH. We can if there's a meeting.

THE RECEPTIONIST FKA JESS. What's the meeting?

DANIEL (*to* THE RECEPTIONIST FKA JESS). The CSR surplus meeting. Hi, I'm Daniel.

DANIEL *offers his hand.* THE RECEPTIONIST FKA JESS *accepts it.*

THE RECEPTIONIST FKA JESS. Hi, I'm – [Jess.]

CLODAGH *(watching the door)*. Sit down then.

THE RECEPTIONIST FKA JESS *sits down and* CLODAGH *slams the door shut.*

CLODAGH *and* DANIEL *resume eating.*

THE RECEPTIONIST FKA JESS *is trying to figure out what's going on. They pick up their spoon.*

DANIEL. Oooh. That looks exotic.

THE RECEPTIONIST FKA JESS. Does it?

CLODAGH. It's rather pungent.

DANIEL. What is it?

THE RECEPTIONIST FKA JESS. Mandarin tagine with couscous and bulgar wheat.

DANIEL. Mandarin like orange?

CLODAGH. No, Daniel. Mandarin, like Chinese.

DANIEL *glares*.

THE RECEPTIONIST FKA JESS *continues eating.*

So do CLODAGH *and* DANIEL.

DANIEL *(to* THE RECEPTIONIST FKA JESS*)*. You're new then?

THE RECEPTIONIST FKA JESS. I suppose so. I've been here about three weeks?

Beat.

Are you new too?

DANIEL. No.

CLODAGH *laughs*.

THE RECEPTIONIST FKA JESS. Oh, sorry. I just haven't seen you before.

CLODAGH. They haven't seen you before, Daniel. Isn't that hilarious?

DANIEL (*to* THE RECEPTIONIST FKA JESS). No... I work from home a lot. I have three small children.

CLODAGH. And?

DANIEL (*exasperated*). And my wife needs a hand!

CLODAGH. Is that a plausible reason?

DANIEL. I'm sorry, what?

CLODAGH. As to why you work from home for weeks on end?

DANIEL. Weeks on...? I'm here at least once a week, Clodagh. What's – [wrong with you?]

CLODAGH. Well the Receptionist has never seen / you.

THE RECEPTIONIST FKA JESS. My name is –

DANIEL. Well that's hardly my fault. She's only been here a few weeks!

CLODAGH. I'm not sure what Crónán would think about that.

THE RECEPTIONIST FKA JESS. Who's Crónán?

DANIEL. See! They don't even know who Crónán is.

CLODAGH. Crónán is the Managing Director.

THE RECEPTIONIST FKA JESS. His name is Crónán?!

CLODAGH. See. They do know who he is.

THE RECEPTIONIST FKA JESS *mimes the name 'Crónán', getting their head around it.*

THE RECEPTIONIST FKA JESS (*to themselves*). I've been calling him Rónán!

CLODAGH *laughs.*

I forwarded a box of protein powder to his house last week under the name 'Rónán'.

Beat.

Can that get me fired?

CLODAGH. He won't like that.

THE RECEPTIONIST FKA JESS. I didn't know. I'm still on probation! Can he fire me for that?

DANIEL *(to* THE RECEPTIONIST FKA JESS*)*. Don't worry about it.

THE RECEPTIONIST FKA JESS. Oh my god.

CLODAGH. Relax. I'm sure you're not the first.

THE RECEPTIONIST FKA JESS. Please don't tell Susan.

HR LADY SUSAN *appears at the glass beside the door. She sees* THE RECEPTIONIST FKA JESS *and it incenses her.*

CLODAGH *seeing this, runs to the door and locks it discreetly. She smiles serenely at an enraged* HR LADY SUSAN, *gives her the thumbs-up and then pulls the blind down.*

CLODAGH. Don't worry about Susan.

DANIEL *(to* THE RECEPTIONIST FKA JESS*)*. She's gas craic, Susan.

CLODAGH. She's carbon monoxide alright.

There's a bang on the door.

The door handle is being lifted up and down from outside.

THE RECEPTIONIST FKA JESS *looks for where the sound came from.*

DANIEL *and* CLODAGH *ignore it.*

They all go back to eating their lunch.

Pause.

THE RECEPTIONIST FKA JESS. What's being discussed? At the meeting? Do I need to have read anything?

DANIEL. Yes.

CLODAGH. No.

THE RECEPTIONIST FKA JESS. Okay...

CLODAGH. We need a quorum for the meeting to proceed and you're... the quorum.

THE RECEPTIONIST FKA JESS. Okay... and what am I the quorum for?

DANIEL. It's a minor Corporate Social Responsibility meeting.

THE RECEPTIONIST FKA JESS. Minor?

CLODAGH. If there's a small amount of money left over from the larger Corporate Social Responsibility budget, Crónán and the Vice-Presidents leave it to us to decide where the money should go to.

THE RECEPTIONIST FKA JESS. And I need to vote on it?

CLODAGH. You need to listen.

THE RECEPTIONIST FKA JESS. Alright.

DANIEL (*to* THE RECEPTIONIST FKA JESS). Have you ever been on a committee before?

THE RECEPTIONIST FKA JESS. In college. I've never really worked in an office before.

DANIEL (*winking*). On the session committee, was it?

THE RECEPTIONIST FKA JESS. The Students' Union.

DANIEL. The union, eh? A bit of collective sessioning for the youths.

THE RECEPTIONIST FKA JESS *pretends that they don't understand*.

Except with sessioning... Instead of bargaining.

THE RECEPTIONIST FKA JESS *still refusing to play along*.

Collective bargaining, collective sessioning...

Beat.

THE RECEPTIONIST FKA JESS. No. I was the postgraduate representative on the Students' Union committee.

DANIEL. Oooh right. Very... impressive.

CLODAGH. You have a masters?

THE RECEPTIONIST FKA JESS. PhD.

Mic drop.

CLODAGH. Excuse me, what?

DANIEL. A PhD.

CLODAGH. You have a PhD?

THE RECEPTIONIST FKA JESS. Yeah, yep.

Pause.

CLODAGH. Well, well, well. A doctor at reception.

DANIEL (*just clocking it*). A doctor?

THE RECEPTIONIST FKA JESS. Yes...

CLODAGH. So you think you're a doctor?

THE RECEPTIONIST FKA JESS. Yes?

CLODAGH. Of medicine?

THE RECEPTIONIST FKA JESS. I never said that.

CLODAGH. I noticed.

DANIEL. Cool. Very cool. What's it in? Your PhD.

THE RECEPTIONIST FKA JESS. Oh, eh, anthropology.

DANIEL. Right. Very intellectual.

An awkward silence.

DANIEL *struggles to come up with a follow-up.*

What kind of anthropology?

THE RECEPTIONIST FKA JESS. Identity mostly. Looking at Western concepts of identity and how they've developed away from more traditional models.

DANIEL *looks at* THE RECEPTIONIST FKA JESS *blankly.*

Well, Western concepts of identity are very much centred on the self whereas non-Western concepts of identity are more about what is shared with others.

CLODAGH. That's a bit too highfalutin for us, isn't it, Daniel?

DANIEL. Very interesting.

An awkward silence.

The Irish aren't caught up in that though, surely? Being centred on themselves? I mean we're always talking about what makes us Irish.

Beat.

Leaving the immersion on and all that.

CLODAGH, *quietly euphoric at this*.

THE RECEPTIONIST FKA JESS *astounded*.

CLODAGH. True. The Irish people love their culture.

THE RECEPTIONIST FKA JESS. That's not really what I'm talking about.

CLODAGH. What are you talking about then?

THE RECEPTIONIST FKA JESS. I don't want to bore you.

CLODAGH. How would *you* talking about *our* identity bore us? I do love being boiled down to stats and figures. Don't you, Daniel?

DANIEL. Well, that depends…

THE RECEPTIONIST FKA JESS. I can assure you. That's not what I do.

CLODAGH (*to* THE RECEPTIONIST FKA JESS). Couldn't you have gotten a more research-based job? Reception seems a little basic for someone with a doctorate.

THE RECEPTIONIST FKA JESS. Not really. I just needed something that paid well with minimal effort. If I'm going to be researching, I'd prefer it be something worth researching.

No point wasting good energy on trying to figure out how to sell people weight-loss gummies or cryptocurrency on the basis of what car they drive.

CLODAGH. I've never sold cryptocurrency or weight-loss gummies. Have you, Daniel?

DANIEL. No.

THE RECEPTIONIST FKA JESS. I didn't mean to suggest you had.

DANIEL. Most of the funds we work for here are entirely reliant on market research. Don't turn your nose up at it too soon. It's an important job.

THE RECEPTIONIST FKA JESS. I'm not. I'd just rather be – [working.]

DANIEL. If we don't know what people want to buy, how do we know what to sell? And if we don't know what to sell, then how do we get people to invest? And if we don't know what people want to invest in then we lose our jobs. And if we lose our jobs –

CLODAGH. That's enough, Daniel.

THE RECEPTIONIST FKA JESS. I understand how it works. I just don't plan on being here long, that's all.

DANIEL and CLODAGH laugh.

DANIEL. I've heard that one before.

CLODAGH. I think I said it myself.

A massive thud is heard against the door.

We hear HR LADY SUSAN grunt.

Before THE RECEPTIONIST FKA JESS can say anything, DANIEL jumps in.

DANIEL. Eh… and what is it like working… under… eh… Susan?

THE RECEPTIONIST FKA JESS. Fine.

CLODAGH. Fine?

THE RECEPTIONIST FKA JESS. Yeah. She seems fine.

CLODAGH. Well she might seem fine now, but just you wait. People like HR Lady Susan, they'll butter you up like a piece of toast, because they're on your side, right? Sure why wouldn't they be? Your side is the side with all of the butter on it, but they're not on your side, they're *inside*. They're one of the molars or the canines inside the mouth that's about to eat you up.

CLODAGH *nods at* THE RECEPTIONIST FKA JESS *to confirm they understand*.

But what they don't realise is that they've got a cavity and a fucking damaged nerve. And they're not as secure as they think they are. So they might be gobbling you up now with all of your butter but they could be out on their arse quicker than you can say tooth extraction.

THE RECEPTIONIST FKA JESS. Okay.

DANIEL. Jesus, what did Susan ever do to you?

THE RECEPTIONIST FKA JESS *puts their lunchbox down*.

DANIEL *begins to lick his bowl clean*.

CLODAGH *and* THE RECEPTIONIST FKA JESS *look on, horrified*.

DANIEL *finishes and looks at them*.

I love it when she makes it chunky.

CLODAGH *smiles like she's screaming internally*.

THE RECEPTIONIST FKA JESS (*to* DANIEL). What is it you do here?

CLODAGH *and* DANIEL. Senior Associate.

DANIEL *looks at* CLODAGH *weirdly*.

THE RECEPTIONIST FKA JESS. You're both Senior Associate?

CLODAGH *and* DANIEL. No.

THE RECEPTIONIST FKA JESS. Okay…

CLODAGH. I'm Crónán's Executive Assistant.

DANIEL. But soon to be an Assistant Vice-President.

THE RECEPTIONIST FKA JESS. Right.

CLODAGH *throws* DANIEL *a filthy look.*

DANIEL. Well, it's only a matter of time at this point.

CLODAGH. Is it?

CLODAGH, *disgusted, gets up and throws her rubbish in the bin. She then goes back to her seat and begins to look into her briefcase.*

DANIEL (*confused*).…That's what you told me?

CLODAGH *scowls.*

DANIEL *goes to the door with his soup bowl. He goes to open it and remembers why it's locked and turns around and puts the bowl on top of a cabinet.*

THE RECEPTIONIST FKA JESS *looks at him strangely.*

HR LADY SUSAN *knocks on the door from the corridor.*

DANIEL *knocks on the table to distract.*

Touch wood anyway.

THE RECEPTIONIST FKA JESS. Touch wood?

DANIEL. Touch wood.

CLODAGH *takes three plastic martini glasses out of her briefcase and places each of them on the table.*

THE RECEPTIONIST FKA JESS *is about to say something when* DANIEL *takes out a black bobbed wig and nine toy water guns. He picks one up and polishes it.*

THE RECEPTIONIST FKA JESS*'s anxiety increases.*

DANIEL *aims the gun at the wall. He presses the trigger.*

THE RECEPTIONIST FKA JESS. D... Daniel!

A measly amount of water comes out at the tip of the gun.

DANIEL. It's fine. There's some fizzy water in the press if we run out.

DANIEL *goes and takes out a few bottles from the press. He takes one and leaves the rest on the table. He fills up his water gun.*

CLODAGH *is sorting out some papers. She eventually produces a elaborately painted piece of cardboard and places it on the centre of the table.*

THE RECEPTIONIST FKA JESS *looks over at it.*

DANIEL *takes a bottle of Ballygowan and puts it in the middle of the cardboard.*

THE RECEPTIONIST FKA JESS. I'm sorry, what's happening? Why are there water guns?

CLODAGH *rolls her eyes.*

CLODAGH. Now, can everyone take out their agendas for this quarter's final CSR committee meeting.

THE RECEPTIONIST FKA JESS. But the water gun – / I don't have an agenda?

DANIEL. I didn't print mine off.

CLODAGH *begins to hand out agendas.*

CLODAGH. Now. I informed our Managing Director two weeks ago that there is a surplus in the CSR budget this year and he and the Senior Vice-Presidents have entrusted in me the power to spend it wisely.

DANIEL. The committee.

CLODAGH. Well – [yes, obviously.]

DANIEL. They've entrusted *the committee* with the power to spend it wisely, not you.

CLODAGH. Well, I'm the one they emailed about it.

DANIEL. And you're the one that emailed *them* about it.

CLODAGH. And they didn't CC you, now, did they? Probably forgot you even work here at this point.

DANIEL incensed but nervous, holds his tongue.

Oh don't worry, we haven't forgotten that you're father of the year. Can we move on?

DANIEL. Please.

CLODAGH. Now. Before we begin there's been a slight change to one of the items on the agenda. So if you'd like to cross out my proposal for community break-dance classes that would be great as it's being replaced with something else.

DANIEL is in the process of crossing this out when he stops himself.

DANIEL. What has it been replaced with?

THE RECEPTIONIST FKA JESS. And the water guns?

CLODAGH. What?

THE RECEPTIONIST FKA JESS. Why? Are there… them.

DANIEL (*to* CLODAGH). Why have you changed it?

THE RECEPTIONIST FKA JESS. Is it okay to have them in the office or…?

DANIEL. Answer me, Clodagh.

THE RECEPTIONIST FKA JESS. I don't mean to annoy you or anything it's just –

CLODAGH. Annoy me?

THE RECEPTIONIST FKA JESS. I'm just wondering.

DANIEL. Clodagh, you can't make a change to the agenda that close to the meeting.

CLODAGH (*to* DANIEL). I think I just did.

DANIEL. It's not allowed.

CLODAGH. According to who?

DANIEL. According to... according to it's not allowed.

CLODAGH. Well let's take a vote then. All in favour of the proposed changes?

CLODAGH puts her hand up. She turns to THE RECEPTIONIST FKA JESS *and glares. She uncertainly puts up their hand.*

DANIEL. Dammit.

CLODAGH. The quorum rules.

DANIEL. That's not fair.

The spider phone starts to ring.

CLODAGH. Please, Daniel. It can wait for any other business.

CLODAGH presses the answer button on the spider phone. HR LADY SUSAN's *shadow is behind the blind on her mobile phone.*

HR LADY SUSAN (*voice-over*). Hi Clodagh –

CLODAGH *hangs up the call.*

THE RECEPTIONIST FKA JESS. Was that – [Susan?]

CLODAGH *and* DANIEL. Prank call.

THE RECEPTIONIST FKA JESS. It sounded like – [Susan.]

CLODAGH (*to* THE RECEPTIONIST FKA JESS). Would you do us the honour of spinning the bottle?

THE RECEPTIONIST FKA JESS. Why are we spinning a bottle?

CLODAGH. To start the meeting.

THE RECEPTIONIST FKA JESS.... Okay. And we need to spin a bottle to do that?

CLODAGH *and* DANIEL. Yes.

THE RECEPTIONIST FKA JESS. I'm not sure I understand.

DANIEL. Well, this is the board you see and each member has a symbol on it. This one is me, see? With the gun on it. And this one is Clodagh with the martini glass and this one is Gareth but he's not here today so it doesn't matter.

THE RECEPTIONIST FKA JESS. What is it?

CLODAGH. It's a mask.

DANIEL. A wrestling mask. Anyway one of us spins the bottle around it to see where it lands and that will determine who will go first. Me, Clodagh or Gareth.

THE RECEPTIONIST FKA JESS. Okay…

DANIEL. So you'll spin it?

THE RECEPTIONIST FKA JESS. I… Sure.

CLODAGH. Well hurry up then.

DANIEL. Great.

> THE RECEPTIONIST FKA JESS *spins the bottle like they've never seen a bottle before.*
>
> *They all watch in silence waiting for it to stop.*
>
> *It stops.*

CLODAGH. YESSSS.

> DANIEL *groans.*
>
> CLODAGH *and* DANIEL *each take out a 'Gresham Professional Services' branded day-by-day desk calendar and slam them on the middle of the table. They each have their names written on them.*
>
> *The phone rings. They ignore it.*
>
> CLODAGH *takes a scarf out of her briefcase and drapes it elegantly around her neck. She puts a pair of sunglasses on.*
>
> DANIEL *puts the black bob wig on. He then takes a woman's blouse from his briefcase and puts it on over his shirt.*

He picks up a martini glass. Maybe he looks like a bad imitation of Joan Collins in Dynasty.

When in costume, they pick up their calendars, formally walk towards each other and exchange each other's calendars.

CLODAGH *takes her phone out and presses it.*

SPEAKER (*voice-over*). Clo-da-gggggh's iPhone connected.

DANIEL *takes his phone out and presses it.*

Strider King of Gondor's iPhone connected.

THE RECEPTIONIST FKA JESS *laughs quietly.*

CLODAGH *and* DANIEL *do not break. They sit down on their swivel chairs.*

CLODAGH *presses play on her phone.*

They both reach for the first page of their calendars and rip it off.

Cheesy muzak that sounds similar to a Real Housewives *theme plays.*

CLODAGH *gets up from her chair and poses.*

CLODAGH. I wasn't made Vice-President... I was born one.

THE RECEPTIONIST FKA JESS, *massively confused at this.*

DANIEL *shakes his head dismissively, gets up from his chair and taunts* CLODAGH.

DANIEL. I'm a country gal at heart but my ambition is big city, baby.

THE RECEPTIONIST FKA JESS. What's going on?

CLODAGH *ignores them.*

DANIEL *is torn.*

CLODAGH. Why file nails?

CLODAGH *mimes filing her nails.*

When you can file financial returns?

DANIEL. Asset management?

DANIEL grabs his chest.

Try managing these assets.

CLODAGH. ICAV? I can do but I'd rather have a ca-va with you.

CLODAGH raises a martini glass.

THE RECEPTIONIST FKA JESS. What's an ICAV?

DANIEL and CLODAGH ignore them.

DANIEL. Turning heads? Easy. Try turning SUVs into SPVs.

DANIEL slut-drops or something similar.

THE RECEPTIONIST FKA JESS. STD?

CLODAGH *and* DANIEL. SPV!

CLODAGH and DANIEL both rip a day from each other's calendars.

CLODAGH. My emails are open. Day and night.

CLODAGH winks and opens her mouth.

The phone rings.

THE RECEPTIONIST FKA JESS, *thoroughly freaked out, answers it before they can stop her.*

THE RECEPTIONIST FKA JESS (*to the spider phone*). Hello?

HR LADY SUSAN (*voice-over*). Open this door. NOW.

THE RECEPTIONIST FKA JESS (*to the spider phone*). What door?

CLODAGH hangs up the phone.

HR LADY SUSAN bangs on the door.

CLODAGH gets off the table trying to block THE RECEPTIONIST FKA JESS *but fails.*

THE RECEPTIONIST FKA JESS *tries to open the door but it's locked. They open the blind and see an incensed* HR LADY SUSAN *standing there.*

CLODAGH *turns the music off.*

Hi Susan.

HR LADY SUSAN (*through glass*). Open this door!

THE RECEPTIONIST FKA JESS *looks back at* CLODAGH *and* DANIEL *and then at* HR LADY SUSAN. *Unsure of what's going on.*

THE RECEPTIONIST FKA JESS (*miming to* HR LADY SUSAN). It's locked.

HR LADY SUSAN *sardonically miming that she didn't realise that.*

HR LADY SUSAN (*through glass*). I KNOW!

THE RECEPTIONIST FKA JESS (*to* CLODAGH *and* DANIEL). Why is the door locked?

Beat.

CLODAGH. Because…

DANIEL. Because…

CLODAGH. This is a team-building exercise.

DANIEL.…That we do with new hires.

CLODAGH. To see if they're a cultural fit.

THE RECEPTIONIST FKA JESS. You said it was a meeting?

DANIEL. It is also a meeting.

CLODAGH. That the team-building exercise is taking place during.

THE RECEPTIONIST FKA JESS. Okay.

CLODAGH. After the game, exercise, I mean meeting we, the committee, will give Crónán our appraisal of your performance as a team player during the exercise.

Pause.

THE RECEPTIONIST FKA JESS. And the door is locked?

DANIEL (*unconvincingly*). Well our team have to stay in here until a decision has been made on the meeting and Susan well her team is, her team is out there and they have to get us to evacuate... the room.

THE RECEPTIONIST FKA JESS. Should I have been told about this, earlier, or?

CLODAGH. No... they don't want you to have time to prepare.

DANIEL. This is all about how you think on your feet. Your problem-solving skills and your commitment to the role. So in this round if you break character you have points deducted.

CLODAGH. Each calendar day taken off leaves you a point down. The one with the least breaking points at the end of the meeting, the exercise gets the casting vote.

THE RECEPTIONIST FKA JESS. And how do you win points?

CLODAGH *and* DANIEL. You don't.

HR LADY SUSAN *bangs on the door again and they all look over. She is frothing at the mouth.*

CLODAGH. And if you leave before the vote you fail the assessment.

THE RECEPTIONIST FKA JESS. The assessment?

CLODAGH. The cultural-fit assessment yes.

THE RECEPTIONIST FKA JESS. But I thought it was a team-building exercise?

DANIEL. The company uses all of the assessments as an opportunity for a team-building exercise.

The phone rings again.

HR LADY SUSAN *glares at them as she rings off her mobile.*

THE RECEPTIONIST FKA JESS *looks at* HR LADY SUSAN *and looks back at* CLODAGH *and* DANIEL.

Look at Susan. She's really into this.

CLODAGH. Put a costume on. It won't look good if she thinks you're not getting involved.

THE RECEPTIONIST FKA JESS. Sure.

CLODAGH *finds a pashmina from her briefcase. She fashions it on* THE RECEPTIONIST FKA JESS *as a dress.*

CLODAGH. There we go. Wave to her. Hi Susan!

THE RECEPTIONIST FKA JESS *turns to* HR LADY SUSAN *at the glass, waves and gives her the thumbs-up.*

HR LADY SUSAN *screams in the corridor and walks away.*

CLODAGH *takes Gareth's day-by-day desk calendar from her bag, crosses his name out and writes 'RECEPTIONIST'. She hands it to* THE RECEPTIONIST FKA JESS.

Ready?

DANIEL *nods.*

CLODAGH *presses play on the music.*

They both wait for THE RECEPTIONIST FKA JESS *to say something. Eventually they catch on.*

DANIEL. Do a tagline.

CLODAGH *rips a day from* DANIEL's *calendar.*

DANIEL *rips a day from* CLODAGH's *calendar.*

THE RECEPTIONIST FKA JESS. A what?

DANIEL. A tagline! It'll help you get into character. I'm a country gal at heart but my ambition is big –

CLODAGH *rips another day from* DANIEL's *calendar and one from* THE RECEPTIONIST FKA JESS's.

THE RECEPTIONIST FKA JESS. Okay... Right, sorry. Ehm... I'm the Receptionist...

DANIEL *encourages them to continue.*

CLODAGH *rips another day from* THE RECEPTIONIST FKA JESS*'s calendar.*

And I... receive people.

DANIEL. Clodagh, stop, deducting points. They don't know what they're doing yet.

CLODAGH. Evidently.

THE RECEPTIONIST FKA JESS. I'm the Receptionist. My front desk is... always open.

CLODAGH *glares at* THE RECEPTIONIST FKA JESS *to continue.*

But if you cross it... you will feel the wrath of a thousand suns?

CLODAGH *stops the muzak.*

CLODAGH. Wrong genre.

DANIEL. Totally wrong genre.

CLODAGH. It needs to make sense.

THE RECEPTIONIST FKA JESS. This needs to make sense?

CLODAGH. Make it seem glamorous. Give it some innuendo and then relate it back to reception. You know, I'm the Receptionist –

THE RECEPTIONIST FKA JESS. My name is –

CLODAGH. I'm the Receptionist, I might look idle but my hands are the devil's workshop.

THE RECEPTIONIST FKA JESS. What?!... Okay. I'm the Receptionist. My front desk is always open but due to a high volume of calls we may not always be available... Right now.

DANIEL. Better.

CLODAGH. Do the devil's workshop bit.

THE RECEPTIONIST FKA JESS. No.

CLODAGH. Well, it needs work.

The music changes prompting them to move along.

They sit down.

CLODAGH *starts to pour water into everyone's martini glasses.*

DANIEL. So what's this about?

CLODAGH. Can't a girl just invite her friends to lunch? There's always an ulterior motive with you, Tiffany.

THE RECEPTIONIST FKA JESS. Who's Tiffany?

CLODAGH *rips another day from* THE RECEPTIONIST FKA JESS*'s calendar.*

DANIEL. Well you did mention a proposal, didn't you? Unless the Duke is getting down on one knee again but I'm sure his orthopaedic surgeon would hardly recommend that.

DANIEL *is delighted with himself.*

CLODAGH *is livid.*

THE RECEPTIONIST FKA JESS *is confused and yet understands that* DANIEL *seems to be winning the game somehow.*

CLODAGH. At least he still has his own knees.

CLODAGH *kicks* DANIEL*'s leg under the table.*

DANIEL *swallows a pained groan, regroups, swills his glass and laughs maniacally.*

CLODAGH *joins in.*

THE RECEPTIONIST FKA JESS, *thoroughly weirded out.*

CLODAGH *glares and rips a page from* THE RECEPTIONIST FKA JESS*'s calendar.*

THE RECEPTIONIST FKA JESS *takes a sip from their glass.*

No, no but seriously. In previous years, the CSR surplus has focused largely on the community. Murals on school walls, donations to youth orchestras, Pride parades and giving the kiddies a fun day out. They've all been great but this year, I'm thinking we make a real impact.

DANIEL. Inspiring.

DANIEL swings his swivel chair and throws a look to a non-existent cameraman in a camera confessional manner.

CLODAGH. Show them what we're made of.

DANIEL. Boss bitch!

CLODAGH. We can make a difference!

DANIEL. Amen, sister.

CLODAGH. I think we should save the bees!

DANIEL (*breaking character*). Bees?

CLODAGH rips another day from DANIEL's calendar.

CLODAGH. Bees.

DANIEL. That's your replacement? We've never been allowed to donate to biodiversity charities before. Why would we do it now?

CLODAGH smugly rips another day from DANIEL's calendar.

CLODAGH. Because, time is running out. For the bees. We must act swiftly.

CLODAGH raises her glass.

DANIEL (*camera confessional*). Oh buzz off.

(*Back to* CLODAGH.) Sounds great. What hive you in mind?

THE RECEPTIONIST FKA JESS *snorts*.

CLODAGH rips a page from THE RECEPTIONIST FKA JESS*'s calendar.*

...IN CONFERENCE ROOM 4

CLODAGH (*to* DANIEL). The bees are dying and you're laughing?

DANIEL. A slip of the tongue.

(*Camera confessional*.) Save the bees? There are several wars going on in the Middle East right now but she wants to save the bees? Oh please. Did someone order a delulu juice at table number nine?

CLODAGH *kicks* DANIEL *under the table again*.

DANIEL *rips a day from* CLODAGH*'s calendar*.

THE RECEPTIONIST FKA JESS (*to* CLODAGH). That's a big cause for ten thousand euro.

DANIEL *rips a page from* THE RECEPTIONIST FKA JESS*'s calendar*.

(*Putting on an accent*.) I mean... That's a big cause for ten thousand euro.

CLODAGH. Obviously.

THE RECEPTIONIST FKA JESS. Do you have any specific ideas...?

CLODAGH *swings in her swivel chair to the non-existent cameraman and shakes her head and rolls her eyes*.

DANIEL (*to* THE RECEPTIONIST FKA JESS). Say something mean.

THE RECEPTIONIST FKA JESS. Ehm... no.

DANIEL *rips a day from* THE RECEPTIONIST FKA JESS*'s calendar*.

CLODAGH *rips a day from* DANIEL*'s calendar*.

DANIEL. Well at least stay in character!

CLODAGH *rips another day from* DANIEL*'s calendar*.

CLODAGH. We can do a 'Save the Bees' campaign to raise some extra funds. I'm thinking a black-and-yellow day in work. We'll serve honeycomb and bananas and black tea.

THE RECEPTIONIST FKA JESS. What?

CLODAGH *rips a day from* THE RECEPTIONIST FKA JESS's *calendar.*

CLODAGH. Everyone in the office, we'll all wear black and yellow and eat honeycomb and bananas and drink... black tea. Just for a day.

DANIEL. How dare you. You know full well that I'm a cool summer and yellow is not in my colour palette!

CLODAGH (*camera confessional*). Funny that. Colour palettes didn't seem to matter when she insisted everyone wear green-and-red tartan to the Christmas party.

(*To* DANIEL.) I hear Bergdorf's are having a sale, if you need something.

THE RECEPTIONIST FKA JESS. Is this like a non-uniform day?

CLODAGH *rips a page from* THE RECEPTIONIST FKA JESS's *calendar.*

DANIEL (*camera confessional*). A non-uniform day, what age are we, twelve? Welcome to my life. Is anyone going to tell me what's going on right now?

THE RECEPTIONIST FKA JESS (*to* DANIEL). It just sounds like what used to happen on non-uniform days in school.

DANIEL. Totally!

DANIEL *swivels his chair and shakes his head.*

CLODAGH. I'm not sure if you noticed but we don't wear uniforms.

THE RECEPTIONIST FKA JESS (*looking down at what they are all wearing*). Sure.

Beat.

I assume the money will go to charities? From the surplus and your black-and-yellow day?

CLODAGH. No. The money will go towards buying a big flouncy net so I can wander around the Docklands saving the bees by hand.

DANIEL *rips a page from* CLODAGH's *calendar.*

DANIEL *(camera confessional)*. Somebody better call Vin Diesel because we've got some drama in the house.

THE RECEPTIONIST FKA JESS. So it is going to charities?

The phone rings.

CLODAGH, DANIEL *and* THE RECEPTIONIST FKA JESS *all look to the glass for* HR LADY SUSAN. *She is not there.*

CLODAGH *presses the answer button.*

FRANK *(voice-over)*. Heya, Clodagh?

CLODAGH *and* DANIEL *breathe a sigh of relief.*

CLODAGH. Hi Frank.

FRANK *(voice-over)*. Hiya, yeah, look. I'm after having Susan down with me.

CLODAGH. Oh… really? What did she want?

FRANK *(voice-over)*. Clodagh.

CLODAGH. What did she want, Frank?

FRANK *(voice-over)*. She says you have the door locked up there and it's a fire hazard.

CLODAGH. We don't have the door locked.

FRANK *(voice-over)*. You said that the last time this happened.

CLODAGH. Are you serious? I think she's suffering from paranoid delusions. Why would we lock a door for a lunchtime meeting? I mean, honestly?!

FRANK *(voice-over)*. Hmmmm.

DANIEL. Hi Frank, no door locked here.

FRANK (*voice-over*). Hiya Daniel. Can you check that for me there.

CLODAGH. Why, because I can't be trusted?

DANIEL. No problem at all.

FRANK (*voice-over*). Clodagh.

CLODAGH. Fine.

DANIEL makes footstep noises with his hands against the desk and makes a noise resembling an unlocked door.

DANIEL. No, all doors open here, Frank.

FRANK (*voice-over*). Great. Nice one, Dan. I've a few packages here for the big man, Clodagh, when you're done.

CLODAGH. I'll send the Receptionist down when we're finished.

THE RECEPTIONIST FKA JESS, *like what?*

FRANK (*voice-over*). Eh, okay. And here, go a bit easier on Sue yeah? She's up to ninety down –

CLODAGH *hangs the phone up.*

DANIEL. Phew.

CLODAGH *glares at* DANIEL.

THE RECEPTIONIST FKA JESS. Is Frank part of the team-building exercise too?

DANIEL. What?

CLODAGH. Yes. He's on Susan's team.

THE RECEPTIONIST FKA JESS (*unsure*). Okay.

CLODAGH *presses play on the music again.*

They all sit back down.

DANIEL. Anyway, I for one don't care for bees and I don't see how saving them will benefit our corporation.

CLODAGH. It's not about benefiting our corporation, Daniel. It's about saving an entire species from extinction!

DANIEL *rips a page from* CLODAGH*'s calendar.*

DANIEL *(camera confessional)*. Extinct? I can see more than a few queen bees from where I'm sitting.

DANIEL *mimes a sting.*

THE RECEPTIONIST FKA JESS. I think the destruction of the earth is pretty urgent.

DANIEL *rips a page from* THE RECEPTIONIST FKA JESS*'s calendar.*

CLODAGH. Thank you, Receptionist.

DANIEL *rips a page from* CLODAGH*'s calendar.*

THE RECEPTIONIST FKA JESS. My name is –

DANIEL. So what are we going to do? Give ten grand to a load of nutters who'll glue themselves to beehives? So people can't collect any honey?? Poor old bears, they love the honey. It's not compelling enough and it's not in line with what we normally do.

CLODAGH *(pointing at* THE RECEPTIONIST FKA JESS*)*. They're the one that wants to sellotape themselves to beehives. I haven't said anything of the sort.

THE RECEPTIONIST FKA JESS. Neither did I?

CLODAGH *rips a page from* THE RECEPTIONIST FKA JESS*'s calendar.*

CLODAGH. I picked up on your tone!

DANIEL *(breaking character)*. Honestly, Clodagh. This makes no bloody sense. Sure the surplus went to a muralist last year and now you're trying to save an entire species on what? Ten grand. Are you alright in the head?

CLODAGH *panics momentarily. She throws her martini glass of water in* DANIEL*'s face. And then rips another page from his calendar.*

DANIEL *is sincerely astounded.*

(*Through gritted teeth.*) It's too early for that.

CLODAGH *rips off several pages from* DANIEL*'s calendar.*

CLODAGH. You're not listening to me. I have a plan, If you'd just –

DANIEL *tries to wring out his wet clothes.*

DANIEL. Well map it out then. Be my guest.

CLODAGH. Bees may seem small but their contribution to our ecology is gargantuan. Without the bees we have no flowers, without the bees we've no grain, without the bees we have no meat, without the bees we have no cotton –

DANIEL. Yeah, yeah, yeah. We get it.

CLODAGH. I believe by funding some local projects and startups we can help to revive the bee population and make a real effort towards combatting the climate crisis.

DANIEL (*camera confessional*). I know people talk about a – (*Air-quotes.*) climate crisis. But –

THE RECEPTIONIST FKA JESS. What's that about?

THE RECEPTIONIST FKA JESS *air-quotes.*

DANIEL. I'm in character.

DANIEL *rips off a page from* THE RECEPTIONIST FKA JESS*'s calendar.*

CLODAGH. No, you're not.

CLODAGH *rips off a page of* DANIEL*'s calendar.*

DANIEL. Yes, I am. Tiffany is a Trump supporter. You know that!

THE RECEPTIONIST FKA JESS. Tiffany?

DANIEL. Yesssss?

CLODAGH. Are you a climate denier, Daniel?

DANIEL *rips a page from* CLODAGH*'s calendar.*

DANIEL. I don't deny there is a climate, Clodagh.

CLODAGH. You know what I mean.

CLODAGH *rips a page from* DANIEL*'s calendar.*

DANIEL. I do know what you mean and I'm not denying that temperatures are rising, I'm... Tiffany, is merely saying that temperatures have risen and fallen for thousands of years as have the sea levels.

CLODAGH. Is Tiffany referring to herself in the third person now?

DANIEL. No... She is not.

CLODAGH. Daniel?

DANIEL *rips a page from* CLODAGH*'s calendar.*

CLODAGH *rips a page from* DANIEL*'s calendar.*

THE RECEPTIONIST FKA JESS (*to* DANIEL). You are aware that because of the climate crisis the world is essentially on fire right now?

DANIEL. So you all keep saying.

CLODAGH. Daniel!

DANIEL. This is just my OPINION!

CLODAGH. Well by the sounds of it your opinions are better off working from home in the future.

DANIEL. I thought you'd be happy to see me. We haven't met like this in months.

CLODAGH. And whose fault is that?

DANIEL. You can't blame me for getting angry when you changed your proposal two minutes before the meeting and don't seem to have any set plan in place? What was wrong with the break-dancing project? Last I heard you had Disco Sean lined up for it and all.

CLODAGH. Need I remind you that this is about doing something worthwhile for the future. For our children and their children. And their children's children.

DANIEL. But you don't have any children?

CLODAGH *screams.*

DANIEL *is panicked by this.*

Ehhhhhhhh… Dance break.

DANIEL *presses play on his phone.*

'Sexy and I Know It' by LMFAO plays (or something similar).

DANIEL *begins to dance.*

CLODAGH *tries to calm herself.*

THE RECEPTIONIST FKA JESS *just watches.*

The lights in the room start to go on and off in a slow, methodical way.

CLODAGH *and* THE RECEPTIONIST FKA JESS *turn to see* HR LADY SUSAN *messing with the light switch in the hall.*

She smiles at them, sadistically.

A fan is heard. HR LADY SUSAN *has a remote for the air conditioning and is turning it up.*

CLODAGH *goes over to the console and turns it back down.*

HR LADY SUSAN *turns it back up, and so on.*

THE RECEPTIONIST FKA JESS *stares at* HR LADY SUSAN, *unsure of what to do.*

HR LADY SUSAN, *noticing she's caught* THE RECEPTIONIST FKA JESS*'s attention, begins to encourage them to open the door.*

This hits a nerve.

THE RECEPTIONIST FKA JESS. She wants me to open the door.

CLODAGH. Well obviously she does. Then her team wins the exercise.

THE RECEPTIONIST FKA JESS. I get that. But she really seems to want me to open the door and I really cannot afford to get on her bad side. I need to pass my probation.

DANIEL begins to rip pages from both of their calendars.

CLODAGH. If you want to pass your probation you need to be doing what we're telling you. After all, we're the ones giving Crónán your appraisal. Not Susan. I'd hate to say that you're not a good fit.

THE RECEPTIONIST FKA JESS *sees the logic in this.*

THE RECEPTIONIST FKA JESS. Eh... okay.

CLODAGH. Here, throw a glass of water in Daniel's face. Susan has probably spotted you're not playing properly and thinks she can lure you out for her team. Show her how committed you are.

CLODAGH hands a glass of water to THE RECEPTIONIST FKA JESS.

DANIEL turns off the music.

DANIEL. What?

THE RECEPTIONIST FKA JESS. I don't want to.

CLODAGH. Just do it. It's fun.

DANIEL. For you maybe.

CLODAGH rips a page from DANIEL's calendar.

CLODAGH. You can shout something out too if you like, when you're doing it. As assessors we're easily impressed by that.

THE RECEPTIONIST FKA JESS. ...I think I should open the door.

CLODAGH. Well then you don't want to pass your probation.

HR LADY SUSAN *is still smiling at* THE RECEPTIONIST FKA JESS. *Willing her on.*

THE RECEPTIONIST FKA JESS. I don't know…

CLODAGH. Why?

THE RECEPTIONIST FKA JESS. Can I just talk to Susan about this?

CLODAGH. No.

DANIEL. Then she'd win.

CLODAGH. And we'd lose. Do you not trust us or something?

THE RECEPTIONIST FKA JESS.… No?

CLODAGH. I'm sorry, what?

THE RECEPTIONIST FKA JESS. I want to go out.

CLODAGH. No.

THE RECEPTIONIST FKA JESS. You have to let me out. I'll make a complaint. This isn't allowed.

CLODAGH. Oh, is it not allowed? Are you going to tell on me, are you? To Her Royal Lady Susan? Will HR be angry? Will I get a telling off? For holding a Managing Director-approved CSR committee meeting? All because you told on me and you have a PhD? Because who am I? Sure I'm just the person who helped make them over fifteen million euro in billable hours last year. What am I to them? I'll tell you what I am to them. I am the life's blood of this organisation. The arteries that keep it pumping and the brain that signals everything and everyone where to go. Crónán doesn't blow his nose without me knowing about it and he wouldn't know how to, if I hadn't shown him. So you might think you have a leg to stand on here but if I want to spend my lunch break running around this boardroom in the nip while doing the Macarena then that's what I'm going to do. Capeesh?

THE RECEPTIONIST FKA JESS *throws the glass of water in* CLODAGH'*s face*.

CLODAGH, *stunned*.

HR LADY SUSAN, *a mixture of horrified and delighted, leaves.*

THE RECEPTIONIST FKA JESS. I'm, I'm sorry. I don't know why I did that.

DANIEL. Well, it's worked anyway. Susan is gone.

CLODAGH *begins to wring out her clothes.*

THE RECEPTIONIST FKA JESS, *guiltily, looks to see* HR LADY SUSAN *is gone.*

CLODAGH. Well thank god for that.

THE RECEPTIONIST FKA JESS. I'm sorry.

CLODAGH. For what? Get over it.

DANIEL *rips off several pages from* CLODAGH*'s calendar.*

DANIEL. BOOYAH! You're down twenty-five breaking points in your own round. It's time to spin the bottle, baby.

(*He spins the bottle.*) Whoop.

CLODAGH. They're not breaking points. I was explaining to her. That doesn't count.

DANIEL. It certainly counted when I was explaining earlier.

DANIEL *takes out a 'Gresham Professional Services'-branded hypothermia blanket (it looks like tin foil) from his briefcase. He puts it on like a cape.*

DANIEL *presses play on his phone. 'The Man Who Sold the World' by Midge Ure or something similar begins playing.*

He picks up one of the water guns and begins patrolling.

Pew pew.

DANIEL *stands swaying from side to side as if he is a character in a video game.*

THE RECEPTIONIST FKA JESS *and* CLODAGH *both turn around to look at* DANIEL.

CLODAGH. Daniel!

DANIEL *walks animatronically towards the table and rips a page from* CLODAGH's *calendar.*

Fine. Come on then.

CLODAGH *and* DANIEL *exchange their calendars. The game is changing where they have to mind their own calendars while also trying to get their opponents. Maybe it's like a game of Capture the Flag.*

CLODAGH *takes out a few hats from her briefcase, looking for one in particular: a 'Gresham Professional Services'-branded beanie. She finds it and puts it on. She rolls down the band to reveal it's been turned into a balaclava. She takes up a water gun and hides under the table.*

DANIEL (*still swaying*). Are you still playing?

THE RECEPTIONIST FKA JESS *just stands there and stares.*

(*Still swaying.*) Are you still playing?

CLODAGH (*from under the table*). Yes.

DANIEL *marches animatronically around the room.*

DANIEL. Well, soldier, the Plutus Province reaches out as far as the eye can see. Can you see it too?

DANIEL *faces the audience, he sways from side to side waiting for the audience to respond.*

THE RECEPTIONIST FKA JESS. Plutus Province?

DANIEL. Are you still playing?

THE RECEPTIONIST FKA JESS.... Yes.

DANIEL *turns to face* THE RECEPTIONIST FKA JESS.

DANIEL. Your mission is to find and disarm the infidel by any means necessary. Do you wish to proceed?

THE RECEPTIONIST FKA JESS *looks back at the glass, to check that* HR LADY SUSAN *is gone. They look at* CLODAGH *hiding and then back at* DANIEL.

THE RECEPTIONIST FKA JESS. Think on my feet…

DANIEL. DO YOU WISH TO PROCEED?

THE RECEPTIONIST FKA JESS (*light bulb*). Video games!

THE RECEPTIONIST FKA JESS *spots a 'Gresham Professional Services'-branded red baseball cap that* CLODAGH *has taken out of her briefcase. They take it and sit down.*

DANIEL *and* CLODAGH *circle the table, trying to get to the other's calendar, while also trying to protect their own.*

THE RECEPTIONIST FKA JESS *grabs a Post-it and writes something.*

DANIEL. In this solemn hour it is a consolation to dwell upon our consistent efforts for charity. But faced with most egregious circumstances this is not a question of fighting for one charity or another but about fighting for what is best and what is right and for those reasons, I would like to propose that this year the surplus of Gresham Professional Service's CSR budget go to Offaly's very own Shannon Cross GAA Club.

THE RECEPTIONIST FKA JESS. You're dressed like a soldier.

DANIEL. Is there a problem?

DANIEL *shoots at* THE RECEPTIONIST FKA JESS.

THE RECEPTIONIST FKA JESS. I just thought you'd say something else, that's all.

DANIEL. I don't see why.

CLODAGH. We have ten thousand euro to donate to a worthwhile cause, Daniel.

DANIEL. And it's not worthwhile enough for you, is it not?

DANIEL *shoots at* CLODAGH.

THE RECEPTIONIST FKA JESS *puts the red hat on. It has a Post-it with a big 'M' stuck on it.*

THE RECEPTIONIST FKA JESS. It's-a-me, Je–

CLODAGH. You mentioned wars in the Middle East earlier?

DANIEL. So? I mean, *So!*

DANIEL *shoots at* CLODAGH.

CLODAGH *shoots at* DANIEL.

THE RECEPTIONIST FKA JESS. So?! You want to give the money to a sports club.

DANIEL *stands up and falls in slow motion dramatically as if he has been hit.*

He lies on the ground.

THE RECEPTIONIST FKA JESS *waits.*

There is no response.

DANIEL *coughs elaborately.*

THE RECEPTIONIST FKA JESS (*jumps up and down out of her seat*). Ba-ding.

DANIEL. Do it with what you said earlier.

CLODAGH *rips a page from* DANIEL's *calendar.*

THE RECEPTIONIST FKA JESS. Fine. You want to give the money to a sports club.

Jumps up and down out of her seat.

Ba-ding.

DANIEL *lifts his head again.*

DANIEL. It's not a sports club.

Beat.

It's a GAA club.

THE RECEPTIONIST FKA JESS (*bending over the table to respond*). It doesn't matter if it's a GAA club, I still don't see how it's a decent and charitable cause.

DANIEL. Where do you get off saying that? You don't know the first thing about it. You were calling it a sports club a minute ago.

DANIEL, *receiving new life, regenerates from the floor.*

Pew.

DANIEL *shoots his water gun.*

THE RECEPTIONIST FKA JESS. Because it is a sports club?

DANIEL. A sports club?!

DANIEL *is hit on his left shoulder.*

A *sports* club?!

DANIEL *is hit on his right shoulder.*

The GAA is your heritage. It's everyone's heritage. It's a symbol of what the Irish are capable of. How they can take a football and fix it with flair and fury. And it is one of the only links left to a world that's fast disappearing!

THE RECEPTIONIST FKA JESS. I... don't know what that means.

DANIEL. It means that it's important and it deserves your undivided attention.

CLODAGH. Don't waste your time, Daniel. Unless it's going to get them a few letters after their name, they're not engaging.

DANIEL *gives* CLODAGH *a look.*

Pew!

CLODAGH *shoots at* THE RECEPTIONIST FKA JESS.

DANIEL *reacts as if a bomb has gone off.*

DANIEL (*to* THE RECEPTIONIST FKA JESS). You've been hit, soldier.

THE RECEPTIONIST FKA JESS. I feel fine.

DANIEL. YOU'VE BEEN HIT, SOLDIER.

THE RECEPTIONIST FKA JESS. Nope.

DANIEL. Yes.

> DANIEL *stands up, threateningly.*

> THE RECEPTIONIST FKA JESS *stands up too.*

> Do you have any idea how bad things are getting in the Midlands?

THE RECEPTIONIST FKA JESS. This has nothing to do with the Midlands.

DANIEL. Of course you don't. Too caught up in your little Dublin bubble. Both of you.

CLODAGH. Daniel, you live in Dundrum.

DANIEL. Yes, I know. Of course. But I'm from Shannon Cross.

CLODAGH. And? Are you not in a bit of a Dublin bubble of your own?

DANIEL. No.

CLODAGH. No?

> CLODAGH *is suspicious. She captures* DANIEL's *calendar and rips a page from it, and begins to take aim at him with her gun.*

DANIEL. No.

CLODAGH. Why are you not in a Dublin bubble, Daniel?

DANIEL. Because… my heart is in Offaly.

CLODAGH. Your heart?

DANIEL. Yes.

> *Keeping the gun on him, she rips another page from his calendar.*

DANIEL *captures* CLODAGH*'s calendar but is getting anxious now.*

CLODAGH. You know, you've been working from home a lot more over the past few months. Why is that?

DANIEL. Because of the kids, Clodagh. You know that. The children.

CLODAGH. How long is it to Dublin? From Shannon Cross.

DANIEL *doesn't respond.*

It's just a question. An hour? Hour and a half? How long does it take in let's say, rush hour? Early-morning commute?

DANIEL. I... can't say I know... that.

CLODAGH. Hmmm.

DANIEL. What?

CLODAGH. Nothing, just wondering. You were saying, specifically your heart is in Offaly?

CLODAGH *aims her water gun at* DANIEL.

DANIEL. Yes, that's what I was saying. And I was saying, that since the closure of the Bord Na Móna fuelled power plants, the economy in the Midlands is plummeting. You can't take away their biggest industry and not provide something to replace it. They let go of more than half of their workforce. And less workers means less customers for local businesses. Delis left without lunch orders, dairies left without milk orders, pubs left without rounds. And GAA clubs left without equipment and jerseys, as less money in the community means less sponsorship. You might look at me talking about this as if it's all a load of country-bumpkin shite but the GAA, in small communities, gives them something to celebrate and something to be proud of. And without sponsorship for jerseys, helmets, mouth guards and sliotars they're as extinct as the power plants and the bees you won't stop going on about.

CLODAGH. Wow, you seem to know a lot about these effects on the community, Daniel. You seem very familiar.

DANIEL. What's that supposed to mean?

CLODAGH. Just that you know a lot.

DANIEL. My family is there.

CLODAGH. Your wife and three kids?

DANIEL. Yes, I mean, no. My mother and my brothers. They're all there.

CLODAGH. You sound a bit confused. Doesn't he sound a bit confused, Receptionist?

THE RECEPTIONIST FKA JESS. *I'm* a bit confused.

CLODAGH. Sounds to me like you might be, I don't know, call me crazy, living there?

DANIEL. No! I am not!

CLODAGH. No need to get angry, Daniel. I was just asking.

THE RECEPTIONIST FKA JESS. Do you play GAA, Daniel?

Beat.

DANIEL. Me? No, no. Not really my thing. The only thing I ever played really was *Metal Gear Solid… Halo… Rayman, Zelda… Call of Duty, Streets of Rage, The Last of Us, The Last of Us Two, Red Dead Redemption, Red Dead Redemption Two*, a little *Street Fighter* –

CLODAGH *starts shooting at* DANIEL.

THE RECEPTIONIST FKA JESS. Right.

DANIEL. My daughter does though, play Gaelic football.

Aha! CLODAGH *zones in on* DANIEL.

CLODAGH. And who does she play for?

DANIEL *panics. He crouches down.*

DANIEL. Watch out, soldier, we're under attack.

CLODAGH. Who does she play for, Daniel?

DANIEL. Pew, pew. Boooooooooom chhhhhhhhhhhhh.

DANIEL *mimes a bomb dropping*.

CLODAGH. Does she play for Shannon Cross?

DANIEL. Yes...

CLODAGH. So you've moved back to Shannon Cross?

DANIEL. I didn't say that, I just said she played for their GAA team!

CLODAGH. And why is she playing for a team in Offaly, then. If she's living in Dundrum? That's what I want to know.

DANIEL. Better coaching.

CLODAGH. Better coaching but they can't afford to buy jerseys?

DANIEL. Yes.

DANIEL *shoots,* CLODAGH *dodges*.

CLODAGH. So you're telling me you drive up and back to Offaly a couple of times a week so your daughter can kick a ball around a field?

CLODAGH *shoots and makes a grab for* DANIEL*'s calendar.* DANIEL *gets there just in time*.

DANIEL. Well, I'm not going to explain it to someone who has no appreciation for the ancient sports of their ancestors.

CLODAGH. Crónán likes GAA. We had a box for the All-Ireland last year. Not sure how he'd feel about funding a team outside of Dublin. He might have a lot of questions about it.

DANIEL. Where are you coming from with this, Clodagh? Don't –

CLODAGH *begins to circle* DANIEL. *He resists it.*

CLODAGH. Don't what? Don't tell Crónán that we're funding a team in Daniel's new neighbourhood in Offaly? I'll have to say something. Or else it might seem like I haven't paid enough attention and by the sounds of things you've upped sticks from Dublin without telling anyone. Which I'm pretty sure isn't allowed. I mean management would at least need to know where you're living so in future, you know, they can take it into account for your next promotion.

DANIEL. I'm not living there, Clodagh. You can't tell him that.

CLODAGH. I'm not buying it and if I'm not buying it, you can be sure that Crónán won't be buying it either.

DANIEL. Well he won't if it's coming from you anyway!

THE RECEPTIONIST FKA JESS. Why can't he live in Offaly?

DANIEL. I'M NOT… living in Offaly, okay?

CLODAGH. Management wouldn't like it. It's not a fireable offence but it might make you seem less trustworthy, less available, less promotable.

CLODAGH *shoots at* DANIEL. *He shoots back.*

THE RECEPTIONIST FKA JESS. Because you don't live in Dublin?

CLODAGH *and* DANIEL. Yes.

DANIEL *considers his options.*

DANIEL. I mean no! I mean yes! I *do* live in Dublin. And Clara, my daughter, she *was* playing for a team up here but we had to move her after I got in a bit of bother, with one of the other coaches. So she does play in Offaly but we haven't moved there… yet.

CLODAGH. I still don't buy it.

DANIEL. You don't have to buy it. There's nothing to buy.

CLODAGH. I'm telling Crónán.

CLODAGH *shoots at* DANIEL *and then presses a button on the spider phone.*

DANIEL. No you're not.

DANIEL *shoots back.*

CLODAGH. Yes, I am.

DANIEL. I haven't moved anywhere!

CLODAGH. Might have disclose this to HR Lady Susan too. Get everyone involved.

CLODAGH *starts to dial a number.*

DANIEL. STOP IT! STOP IT NOW! MY DAUGHTER IS ONLY PLAYING IN OFFALY SO I COULD ESCAPE A CRIMINAL CHARGE.

CLODAGH *presses the hang-up button.*

CLODAGH. What?

THE RECEPTIONIST FKA JESS *takes a few steps back as if they're scared of him.*

DANIEL. It sounds worse than it is. It's not like that.

CLODAGH. It sounds like you might be a criminal.

DANIEL. I'm not! I'm not! I just got… I got carried away. That's all. Clara started playing football when she was about five. And she was brilliant, she was a star. Everyone could see it. Strange for me, considering I'd never been much interested in sports. But I started coaching her team anyway. Good dad and all that. I had never really felt comfortable in Dublin but I came up at eighteen for college and never went back. Was never expected to come home, come home for what? But being in that clubhouse made me feel grounded, I suppose. Not that it reminded me of home just that it made me feel like I belonged somewhere. And Clara was getting better, the best for her age. She's so good they want her on the under-elevens. And I'm disappointed at first. It was our thing that we used do together but it's flattering and a big deal and she wants to do it so I let her. And the coach on the other team, Galvo, is a real Dub, not like you, or you either. He's played county, will have his ashes sprinkled on Hill 16. That kind of Dub. But even without Clara my team is still doing good, they're great. And the under-elevens aren't bad either, Clara is the best on the pitch and your man Galvo is just an out-and-out dose. Giving me tips on my team, ball control, free kicks. He was on a Dublin development squad when he was twenty and thinks he made the GAA. And I grin and bear it for a while, I don't mind. My team are at the top of their league and his are straggling behind in their own and so what does he know? Everything apparently. He congratulates me one day on our successes, tells me if I want us to stay there that I need to focus on my back line, take the focus off goal-scoring and I can't take it any more.

DANIEL *backs away from the table, takes out his water gun and aims it at a point in the audience.*

'We're grand, thanks.'

DANIEL *shoots at the audience.*

And he looks at me, swaggering like he's Conor McGregor. 'Yoo're reel full of yerself aren't ye?' 'Maybe,' I say. 'Who wants to know?' He does, evidently. We arrange for the under-tens and under-elevens to play a 'friendly', a good contest for both of them. And I'm giving it everything, to put this Dublin prick in his place. To show the capital everything I've felt for the past eighteen years. This is for your shitty transport system, pew! This is for the centralisation of public services and government structures, pew! This is for your nepotistic private-school hierarchy, 'What school did you go to, son? St Boggers?' Kapow! This is for walking around like the spire is stuck up your arse, pew! This is for the abandonment of rural Ireland and the lack of industry and facilities in place to keep it going, driving everyone and everything out and forcing them into cities not big enough to take them and jobs that would make a leaf-blowing competition seem interesting!!

Beat.

If Galvo has his girls out training at eight a.m., I have mine out training at seven. Which means Clara's already been doing a run around before her 'coach' arrives, which means

I've already managed to one-up his reputation. His aggression towards me getting less and less passive as the weeks go on. We set a date. Sunday the fifteenth of April. Perfect. I'm ready to go, my girls are ready to go and I'm so distracted by the game that I forget that we're due to go for dinner in my mammy's that day. Will we have to cancel, Clara asks? No... I say... Granny has been working hard on it. Ham, cabbage, white sauce, roasted potatoes, boiled potatoes, mash, sprouts, there'll probably be soup too, maybe even ice cream and you'll need a good feed before the match. Okay, she says; great, I say. If it's what she wants then that's what we'll do.

On the morning of the match we wake up early and get on the road to Offaly. We drive through the county and I show Clara her homeland. This is where you would have grown up, I say. If your mammy and daddy didn't have to be chained to a desk for forty-eight hours a week. If they weren't so possessed by their pay cheques and fancy holidays. If they'd stayed true to themselves and their counties, this is where you could have grown up. She knows, she says. We visit Granny once a month. We arrive at Mammy's house and she's already got the dinner on the table. Eat up, I tell Clara. The match is at three and it's twelve p.m. now. 'Eat up and fuel those legs of yours. If you eat it all, there'll be a prize on the way home.' It's at this point, I'm not really sure what I'm doing any more but halfway back to Dublin with an hour to go to throw-in we stop off in a service station to claim her prize for eating her meat and three veg. She asks for Rolos and I buy them.

DANIEL *shoots water from the water gun.*

She asks for Dip Dabs and I buy them.

DANIEL *shoots again.*

Haribo Tangfastics.

DANIEL *shoots again.*

Haribo Starmix.

DANIEL *shoots again*.

Peanut M&Ms.

DANIEL *shoots again*.

Peanut Butter M&Ms.

DANIEL *shoots again*.

Brownie M&Ms.

DANIEL *shoots again*.

Salted Caramel M&Ms.

DANIEL *shoots again*.

Mint M&Ms.

DANIEL *shoots again*.

Crispy M&Ms.

DANIEL *shoots again*.

Mini M&Ms.

DANIEL *shoots again*.

Hi-Protein M&Ms.

And I buy them. I buy them all like I've lost control and she's loving it. Everything her nine-year-old heart could wish for and what am I doing? But I can't stop. She's milling them all into her gob at the back of the car and I know this can't end well, won't end well, not after boiled ham, coagulated cabbage and three courses of spuds. But I can't stop her. I'm trying to get the words out of my mouth but they stay there, silent. We arrive at the pitch with only minutes to spare. 'Gerrout here,' Galvo screams at Clara, who's beginning to look green in the face from all of the spuds, sweets and the motion of the car. The match starts and it's neck-and-neck. The elevens are bigger but the tens are faster. Galvo is screaming at Clara now saying all sorts to her from the side of the pitch. She was slow during the first half, I had hoped as much. But in the second she can barely keep her eyes open and her team are feeling the heat. And I know I've gone too far, because she looks like she's about to blow and Galvo looks like a vein is about to pop in his forehead. Clara falls down after a slight push from a left back, her cheeks now swelling with regurgitated syrup, ham, mash and roasties when it all comes thundering out. Vomit everywhere. Galvo storms onto the pitch. 'Gerrup. Gerrup NOW.' He grabs her by the arm and I'm off like a light. 'Take your hands off my daughter, you fucking ogre.' We're circling each other now, like fighter jets ready to make a hit. 'What have ye done to her? She's a bleedin' athlete, she needs her greeuns.' He shouts, as Clara vomits up a lollipop with the stick still intact. 'She ate her greens in Offaly. Or are Offaly greens not good enough for you?' I growl, momentarily forgetting that I poisoned my own daughter with sugar and trans fats for a good two hours this afternoon. 'What's a green in Offaly, cowshite? Youse muck savages could do with reading a book or two' and I BANG.

DANIEL *shoots water from the water gun that then falls lamely to the ground.*

DANIEL *is out of the story now. He hangs his head in shame.*

THE RECEPTIONIST FKA JESS. What did you do?

CLODAGH. Ssh.

THE RECEPTIONIST FKA JESS. What happened?

DANIEL *doesn't respond.*

Did you kill him? Galvo?

DANIEL. No, I didn't kill him. Jesus.

THE RECEPTIONIST FKA JESS *gestures towards the gun.*

THE RECEPTIONIST FKA JESS. Sorry.

DANIEL. I hit him so hard he falls over. The girls are all running off scared, scared of me and what I've turned myself into. Clara's still vomiting and the other parents are beginning to form what looks like an angry mob so I grab her and run away.

Run away from them and whoever it is I've become. We get banned and not just from the club. Galvo says he won't press charges as long as we don't show our faces in the Dublin championship again. And that is why my daughter plays football in Offaly.

CLODAGH. So you did move?

DANIEL. No! After that, she starts playing in Shannon Cross. And it just feels right. I drive her up for training and a match twice, three times a week. It feels good. And believe me, Clodagh, as much as it pains me to say it, we haven't moved to Offaly. But if and when we do, I'd prefer that Crónán heard it from me. My proposal isn't about point-scoring. It's about a community in need. That we've all just abandoned and for what? Three-bed semi-ds, a Luas and a Wowburger? I hated it there when I was younger and I hate it here now but by god if I have to be stuck in this place for the rest of my life it might as well be good for something!

CLODAGH. Well if it stops you from poisoning your daughter.

DANIEL. What? No!

CLODAGH. You didn't poison your daughter?

DANIEL. I didn't poison her. I let her eat sweets.

CLODAGH. You let her eat the whole service station by the sounds of it.

DANIEL. I didn't mean to… Something came over me. Don't let Shannon Cross suffer for my mistakes.

THE RECEPTIONIST FKA JESS. The GAA are pretty well funded.

DANIEL. The GAA might be but Shannon Cross aren't. There won't be a team left to play there the way the emigration is going.

CLODAGH. They'll find other teams to play for.

DANIEL. Where? In Timbuktu? What becomes of the Midlands then? The wasteland before time?

CLODAGH. And burning peat was going to end so well for it?

DANIEL. They need this money.

CLODAGH. More like you need this money to ingratiate yourself with your daughter's new coach.

DANIEL. My community needs this money and by god I'm going to get it for them.

CLODAGH. But they're not your community because you left.

DANIEL. No I didn't!

CLODAGH. You didn't leave?

DANIEL recomposes himself.

DANIEL. It is a good cause that will benefit an entire community.

Beat.

CLODAGH. Well we might still have to report you to HR for those fisticuffs on the GAA pitch.

THE RECEPTIONIST FKA JESS. Clodagh...

DANIEL. What on earth would HR have to do with that?

CLODAGH. I'd imagine aggressive behaviour in or out of the workplace is a concern for HR.

THE RECEPTIONIST FKA JESS (*to* CLODAGH). And locking someone in a room against their will *in* the workplace isn't aggressive behaviour?

THE RECEPTIONIST FKA JESS drops an imaginary bomb with her hand on the table in a 'mic drop' fashion. She makes bomb-like noises.

DANIEL. Are you honestly saying this is not a compelling cause? An impoverished local community needs your help. You're telling me it's not worthy?

CLODAGH. For someone who's spent the past five years helping funds invest in the wind farms that 'took' your community down, this really does seem to be a dramatic u-turn.

This has hit a massive nerve.

DANIEL. How dare you? As if I would have worked on them if I had a choice. And pretty rich coming from you, how many bees have you personally slaughtered from all of those pesticides our clients have been pumping into the wild? This is the one time a quarter we get to have fun, Clodagh. I'm not even supposed to be in on Tuesdays but I couldn't wait for this. And all you've done all day is go at me like a terrier. Lucky Gareth and his lucky colon.

CLODAGH *and* DANIEL *glare at each other until* DANIEL *stops abruptly and opens the cabinet doors and takes whatever he can find and lays it around the room as if he's placing ammunition.*

THE RECEPTIONIST FKA JESS. What's going on?

CLODAGH. Surrender.

DANIEL *is not playing any more, his aggression has become very real. He takes a lighter out and starts turning it on and off.*

THE RECEPTIONIST FKA JESS. He's not going to use the lighter, is he?

CLODAGH. What do you think?

THE RECEPTIONIST FKA JESS. Well he used the water gun?!

DANIEL *takes an empty Barry's Tea cardboard box and puts it over his head and moves towards the door as if he is invisible.*

THE RECEPTIONIST FKA JESS *is baffled.*

CLODAGH. A disguise.

DANIEL (*speaking with the cardboard box over his head*). Attention, infidels. You have been captured.

THE RECEPTIONIST FKA JESS. Infidels?

DANIEL, *with the box over his head, starts walking around the boardroom and sticks his hand out and starts clicking his measly Bic lighter.*

DANIEL. Your quarters have been laden with TNT. If you do not give yourselves up these explosives will be detonated in ten, nine, / eight, seven, six, five, five, five, five, five, five, five, five –

The fire alarm goes off.

THE RECEPTIONIST FKA JESS. What do we do?

CLODAGH. Nothing.

THE RECEPTIONIST FKA JESS. The fire alarm is going off.

CLODAGH. Clever move to be fair.

THE RECEPTIONIST FKA JESS. But what if there is a fire?

CLODAGH. The only fire in this office is the one under Susan's arse.

THE RECEPTIONIST FKA JESS (*pointing at* DANIEL's *lighter*). And that is?

DANIEL. Five! Five! Five!

CLODAGH. You think that has set off a building-wide fire alarm?

THE RECEPTIONIST FKA JESS. Well, something has! Give me the key!

DANIEL. Five! Five! Five!

CLODAGH. Yes, five, four, three, two, one. Get on with it, Daniel.

DANIEL. Infidels, abort!

THE RECEPTIONIST FKA JESS. The key, now!

CLODAGH. You'll be marked down on your cultural-fit assessment!

THE RECEPTIONIST FKA JESS. I don't fucking care!

CLODAGH *hands over the key in a blasé manner.*

THE RECEPTIONIST FKA JESS *grabs it and goes to the door. As they put it in the lock the fire alarm begins to slow and quieten until it stops.*

THE RECEPTIONIST FKA JESS *opens the door.*

DANIEL *stops what he's doing and stands beside* CLODAGH.

There is calm for a moment.

THE RECEPTIONIST FKA JESS *takes a step outside.*

HR LADY SUSAN *rounds on her from the right.*

HR LADY SUSAN. WHAT KIND OF ETIQUETTE AND PROCEDURE DO YOU CALL THIS? HOW DARE YOU DEFY –

THE RECEPTIONIST FKA JESS *shuts the door in* HR LADY SUSAN*'s face quickly and jumps back into the room. They lock the door.*

THE RECEPTIONIST FKA JESS. Susan isn't doing the team-building exercise, is she?

CLODAGH. No. Not that she's aware of at least.

THE RECEPTIONIST FKA JESS. She's going to fire me, isn't she?

CLODAGH. No. What would she fire you over?

THE RECEPTIONIST FKA JESS. Oh, I don't know, destroying company property? Creating fire hazards? Lying to the security man?

DANIEL. His name is Frank!

THE RECEPTIONIST FKA JESS. And my name is Jess and I'm about to get fired. Not that any of you seem to care!

CLODAGH. You're not getting fired. You're on your lunch break. She can't tell you what to do on your lunch break. You don't get paid for your lunch break. Do you think we'd do this on company time?

THE RECEPTIONIST FKA JESS. I'll never get a mortgage now. Sam will leave me and why? Because I spent a Tuesday lunch hour shooting water pistols and slut-dropping? What the fuck am I going to do?

DANIEL. If you're getting fired then we're all getting fired and that's not going to happen, now, is it?

THE RECEPTIONIST FKA JESS. I'm still on probation!

Silence.

They regroup.

CLODAGH (*calculating*). Okay, let's just wrap this up then, shall we? Daniel, you're down eighty-two breaking points, in comparison to my fifty-five, that gives you only a fifteen per cent share of the vote whereas mine is thirty-point-two and Jess, with your five... breaking points you're left with a, forty-four-point-eight per cent share of the vote. My, my. Hasn't that worked out well for yourself.

THE RECEPTIONIST FKA JESS. What?

DANIEL. You won.

THE RECEPTIONIST FKA JESS. What did I – How have I won?

CLODAGH. All you have to do now is vote.

THE RECEPTIONIST FKA JESS. Vote?

CLODAGH. You have the deciding vote.

THE RECEPTIONIST FKA JESS. I have to vote?

CLODAGH. Yes. It may be lunchtime but this is a meeting first and foremost. Of which you now have the deciding vote. Which proposal will it be?

THE RECEPTIONIST FKA JESS. Which what?

DANIEL. Our proposals.

DANIEL *and* CLODAGH *look at* THE RECEPTIONIST FKA JESS *earnestly.*

The balls or the bees?

CLODAGH. Balls?

DANIEL *mimes kicking a ball and scoring*.

THE RECEPTIONIST FKA JESS. I have to decide?

CLODAGH. Well I'm hardly going to vote for a GAA club, now, am I?

DANIEL. And I'm hardly going to back something as vague and suspicious as 'Save the Bees'.

CLODAGH (*to* DANIEL). You didn't let me finish.

DANIEL. Oh there was more? Sorry about that, I could have done with a nap.

CLODAGH. Is it naptime at home on the farm? What's the time zone difference in Offaly, it must have been a long drive up this morning.

DANIEL. Wow, you're obsessed with it, aren't you? Every little thing about this place and every person inside of it. You have nothing else going on for yourself, so you consume yourself with all of it. What a sad little life you must lead if this is what you do to make yourself feel good.

CLODAGH. Believe me, I don't spend a second of my day wasting time on anything to do with you.

THE RECEPTIONIST FKA JESS *tries to get in between the two of them*.

DANIEL. And thank god for that.

They can't.

CLODAGH. Waltzing in here jumping up the career ladder while your wife minds, how many is it now? Three, four kids, why not? Sure you can still work from home while you're climbing. And why is that so important anyway? So there'll be someone to hold the baby if your wife needs to take a shit?

DANIEL. How dare you. My wife doesn't shit!

CLODAGH. Well she certainly takes enough of it!

THE RECEPTIONIST FKA JESS. Shut up. Both of you. I've had enough of this.

DANIEL. You have to vote on something!

THE RECEPTIONIST FKA JESS. Well I'm not voting on these!

CLODAGH. Do you have a better idea?

THE RECEPTIONIST FKA JESS. YES!

CLODAGH. Go on then.

THE RECEPTIONIST FKA JESS. Well... There's loads of things... that would be better.

CLODAGH. Yes, there are loads of things. Now what are you suggesting?

THE RECEPTIONIST FKA JESS. Eh... Homeless charities.

CLODAGH. Can't do that, it'll seem like we're taking accountability for the role the funds we work for play in the housing crisis.

THE RECEPTIONIST FKA JESS. We work for them?

CLODAGH. Yes, next?

THE RECEPTIONIST FKA JESS. How do we work for them?

CLODAGH. We run their companies obviously or did you find the Student Accommodation Fund too opaque a title?

THE RECEPTIONIST FKA JESS. Oh.

DANIEL. What did you think it was?

THE RECEPTIONIST FKA JESS. I... don't know.

CLODAGH. Did you think it was a charity?

THE RECEPTIONIST FKA JESS. ... Maybe.

DANIEL (*to* CLODAGH). Better not tell them about the German Pension Funds so.

THE RECEPTIONIST FKA JESS. What about the German Pension Funds?

CLODAGH. They own a lot of the 'Build to Let' projects in Dublin.

THE RECEPTIONIST FKA JESS. German Pension Funds?!

DANIEL. Yes and we work for them, tangentially but still. I thought you were supposed to be the one with the PhD. Do you not read the news no?

THE RECEPTIONIST FKA JESS. Of course I do… I just didn't know this place was employed by them. I've only been here three weeks.

CLODAGH. Ah-ah-ah. Not employed. Contracted.

THE RECEPTIONIST FKA JESS. Isn't that the same thing?

CLODAGH *and* DANIEL. No.

DANIEL. Next idea?

THE RECEPTIONIST FKA JESS. …Cancer research?

DANIEL. No, no, no. Some of our clients are involved with Big Pharma, they won't like that.

CLODAGH. Next?

THE RECEPTIONIST FKA JESS. Medical aid for Palestine?

CLODAGH. Well someone's never been to our office in Tel Aviv.

DANIEL. Clearly.

THE RECEPTIONIST FKA JESS (*to* DANIEL). But you mentioned the Middle East – [earlier.]

DANIEL. I was in character.

CLODAGH. I thought Tiffany voted for Trump.

DANIEL *tries to brush this off*.

THE RECEPTIONIST FKA JESS. Okay well what about domestic violence then? A women's shelter?

CLODAGH. Oh no.

DANIEL. Not a good idea.

CLODAGH. One of our board members was involved in a bit of trouble a few years ago. If we make a donation to something like that the press might find out and make a big thing out of it.

THE RECEPTIONIST FKA JESS. 'A big thing out of it'?

Beat.

'A bit of trouble'?

DANIEL. Yes.

CLODAGH (*to* THE RECEPTIONIST FKA JESS). Hell, I'm as angry as you are but it's better the money go to *something* instead of profits.

THE RECEPTIONIST FKA JESS. What about poverty?

CLODAGH. No, that's not a good look.

THE RECEPTIONIST FKA JESS. 'Not a good look'?

CLODAGH. Yes well it's drawing attention to the social and economic inequalities in Irish society and we need to be advertising Ireland as a place of wealth and dominance for potential clients. And a photo shoot in a soup kitchen is hardly going to do that, now, is it?

THE RECEPTIONIST FKA JESS *is reaching boiling point. Breathing heavily and grunting.*

DANIEL (*to* CLODAGH). We've been there.

THE RECEPTIONIST FKA JESS *gets up on the table and screams.*

THE RECEPTIONIST FKA JESS. Raaaaaaaargh!!!!!

CLODAGH *and* DANIEL *watch on.*

CLODAGH. How are you getting on there?

THE RECEPTIONIST FKA JESS. WHAT IS THIS PLACE?

DANIEL. Gresham Professional Services.

THE RECEPTIONIST FKA JESS. AND YOU'RE OKAY WITH THAT?

DANIEL. I mean they pay my bills. I have three kids.

THE RECEPTIONIST FKA JESS. Yes, you have three kids, you've told us!

Beat.

Move out of home they said, pay obscene rents they said, get a mortgage they said, give up your hopes and dreams they said, just for six months they said. Just until permanency they said. Then we'll give you a mortgage, they said. Don't work too hard they said, just something that's over forty K they said, reception they said, that'll be easy, I said, can save my energy for research and publishing, I said.

Only six months they said, need to pass probation they said, academia not a real job they said, not real money for the banks they said. What? Is it Monopoly money, I said? Laugh, they did but don't say no, they don't. Don't spend, they said, not for six months, or at least take money out of ATMs so they can't see what you've spent, they said. Maybe a hundred a week, for groceries, bills, travel and fun. But maybe don't have fun, not for six months anyway, they said. So I'll do what you say I said. And I end up here and your one says sit out there she says. Answer the phone she says, do the post she says, book the couriers she says, make the tea she says. I am a doctor of science and anthropology specialising in Western concepts of identity in the twenty-first century, I said. Shut up and make the tea, she says. No, I said. Do you want to pass your probation, she says. Do the woods shit in the pope I said. Well go she said. Fine I said. I won't, I said. And then you and the martini glasses and the wigs and the – Dress up! You said. Do this you said. Dance you said and the guns you said, more guns you said and the lighter how do you explain the lighter?! We can't give money to this because we're benefiting from cancer, we can't give money to that because a domestic abuser might start crying and we can't give it to people who really need it because that might make us look culpable. I SWEAR TO GOD, WHERE AM I AND WHY THE FUCK IS IT HADES?!?!

Silence.

CLODAGH *tentatively pushes the bottle towards* THE RECEPTIONIST FKA JESS.

CLODAGH. Spin the bottle. It'll help.

THE RECEPTIONIST FKA JESS *looks at her blankly.*

DANIEL. It helps let out a lot of steam. Sure this whole thing only started one day when I accidentally gave Gareth a finger-gun during an AGM. By the end of it, Clodagh had thrown her Perrier on top of me and Gareth had been turned into a gelatinous cube.

It felt good, like it wasn't real but it was and it was fun. We almost never get to do meetings just the three of us but when they're at lunchtime and on our watches we do whatever the hell we like with them.

CLODAGH. And now the power is yours. So what would you like to do with it?

THE RECEPTIONIST FKA JESS *is listening. She picks up the board and has a look at it.*

THE RECEPTIONIST FKA JESS. I... don't know.

CLODAGH. You can do anything you want with it.

DANIEL. Or you could do Gareth's.

CLODAGH. Or anything you want. Australian soap opera?

THE RECEPTIONIST FKA JESS. No.

CLODAGH. Musical theatre.

DANIEL. How would that even work?

THE RECEPTIONIST FKA JESS. Can I do – [Gareth's?]

CLODAGH. Something intellectual. Trivial Pursuit?

THE RECEPTIONIST FKA JESS. Eh… no.

DANIEL. Gareth's could work. I think I have a script he wrote from the last time we did it.

CLODAGH. Or we can just end this now. Will we take a vote?

DANIEL. Sure there's no fun in that.

DANIEL finds the script in his briefcase.

Here we go.

THE RECEPTIONIST FKA JESS. It's wrestling, isn't it?

DANIEL. Yes. Do you know it?

THE RECEPTIONIST FKA JESS. I watched a bit when I was younger… I did an essay on Roland Barthes' concept in my undergrad.

Beat.

CLODAGH *and* DANIEL *look at each other blankly.*

DANIEL. Great. Here's the script. Make changes where you need to.

CLODAGH. You're really throwing her into the deep end here. I don't think it's fair.

DANIEL. You don't think it's fair?

CLODAGH. No.

DANIEL. And what about the time we had to do the meeting on Zoom and you made me throw water in the face of my computer screen or there'd be a point deduction?

CLODAGH. Well, according to the rules…

DANIEL. Try explaining that to IT, Clodagh.

CLODAGH. Fine.

(*To* THE RECEPTIONIST FKA JESS.) But I amn't feeling my best. So go easy on me.

THE RECEPTIONIST FKA JESS (*insincerely*). Sure.

DANIEL. Great. It's in your hands now.

DANIEL *hands* THE RECEPTIONIST FKA JESS *the calendars.*

DANIEL *takes* CLODAGH'*s home-made balaclava and puts it on. Then he takes his shirt off. Maybe he has a vest on, maybe he doesn't.*

He puts on some music. 'Gonna Fly Now' (Rocky *theme*) *or something similar.*

CLODAGH *takes her costume from her briefcase. Maybe she puts on glasses, maybe she puts on a blazer, maybe she smears a specific kind of lipstick on her face. Whatever she does, she looks like a bad impression of* HR LADY SUSAN.

CLODAGH *and* DANIEL *begin to stretch.*

They both skulk around the room flexing until THE RECEPTIONIST FKA JESS *catches on.*

Excited, THE RECEPTIONIST FKA JESS *takes her receptionist's headset and puts it on.*

DANIEL *gives them the thumbs-up.*

The music settles.

CLODAGH *and* DANIEL *both look at her like, Ready?*

THE RECEPTIONIST FKA JESS *nods.*

THE RECEPTIONIST FKA JESS (*reading off script*). Weh-weh-weh-welcome folks to Tuesday night's punch hour. It's time for your punch break, ladies and gentleman, so get those punchables out of your punch boxes and strap on in because it's punch time. Howdy there, scout. Howdy back, chief. Howdy, y'all??

DANIEL. That's the other commentator. Here, wear these.

DANIEL *gives* THE RECEPTIONIST FKA JESS *a pair of sunglasses. They put them on.*

THE RECEPTIONIST FKA JESS. Who do we have in the ring tonight, scout?

They take the glasses off.

Oh we have a much-awaited showdown, my oh my do we have a good one here for you tonight. Are y'all ready to rumble?

As indicated in their script they get up and try to rouse the crowd.

I said are y'all ready to rumble? Well that's more like it. Now will you please welcome to the ring… She may have been mean to you by the photocopier, she might have stolen the cake in your lunchbox that had your name on it, she may even have spread a rumour that you smell like gone-off COLESLAW. But she's here today to defend her title of Office Bitch it's…

(*Laughing*.) HR LADY SUSAN??!

DANIEL *presses play on 'The Bitch is Back' (Tina Turner version) or something similar.*

CLODAGH *swallows her discomfort and goes for the character full force. She hisses and growls at the audience. She pounds her hands against her chest like a wrestler and screams, taunting* DANIEL. *She gets up on the table.*

(*Partly scripted, partly off the cuff*.) And now, making their way through the arena, it's their opponent. They may not be here that frequently and they may hate your Dublin accent but… their heart is in the right place and that place is OFFFFAAAAALLLLLY. It's the one, the only, Daniel the Señor Associate!!

DANIEL *presses play on 'Jump' by Van Halen or something similar.*

DANIEL *runs and lunges around the room as if he were carrying the Olympic Torch. He climbs up on the table where he faces* CLODAGH.

CLODAGH *picks up a bottle of water and uses it as a microphone.*

CLODAGH. Daniel, Daniel, Daniel. Has it really come to this? Me HR Lady Susan and you, the Señor Associate being judged, ordered and bossed around by the Receptionist? It's hardly how I envisioned my day going, when I got out of bed this morning, let me tell you.

DANIEL *also picks up a bottle of water and uses it as a microphone*

DANIEL. Well, for starters, Susan. The Receptionist's name is…

THE RECEPTIONIST FKA JESS. Eh, Jess.

DANIEL. Is Jess. And as long as her heart is in the right place, she can boss me around all she wants.

THE RECEPTIONIST FKA JESS *whoops and roars in approval.*

Now, which will it be, the bees? Or the balls of Shannon Cross GAA Club?! I can't hear you?! Which will it be?!

THE RECEPTIONIST FKA JESS *momentarily panics as they deviate from the script.*

THE RECEPTIONIST FKA JESS. Great opening statements here from both HR Lady Susan and the Señor Associate.

She puts the glasses on and begins to go off-book.

Eh… it sure is. This match is going to be a tough call. I love bees! On the other hand, those balls sure do need to be PUMPED UP.

THE RECEPTIONIST FKA JESS *does a dance move.*

DANIEL *and* CLODAGH *nod at her in approval. They wait for her next instruction.*

Oh yeah, right. HR Lady Susan and the Señor are circling each other here. Waiting for one of them to make the first move.

DANIEL *and* CLODAGH *circle for a while waiting for instruction.*

CLODAGH. Today, Jess.

THE RECEPTIONIST FKA JESS. Sorry. Señor lunges.

DANIEL *grunts and lunges.*

CLODAGH *glares at* THE RECEPTIONIST FKA JESS.

But misses!! This is going to be a close one, folks.

CLODAGH *and* DANIEL *go back to circling.*

HR Lady Susan initiating her… special move here. Is she about to… off-board him?

CLODAGH. What is that?

THE RECEPTIONIST FKA JESS. I don't know, I'm thinking on my feet.

DANIEL. Jump up on my back.

CLODAGH. I don't want to.

DANIEL. Well how are you supposed to off-board me when you're not on-board me?

THE RECEPTIONIST FKA JESS. She fails!

They rip a a page from CLODAGH*'s calendar.*

Señor has a chance here to go for it. What will he do…

They scan the script looking for inspo.

Will it be his secret weapon, it might just be. It's time for him to PROJECT management.

DANIEL. Yessssss.

DANIEL *goes to scoop* CLODAGH *up over his shoulder.*

CLODAGH. NO!

DANIEL. What's wrong? We've done this before, Clodagh. I just pick you up and spin you around a few times.

CLODAGH. I don't want you to.

DANIEL. Okay what about the office business trip.

CLODAGH. Definitely not.

THE RECEPTIONIST FKA JESS. You're going to lose a lot of points then.

CLODAGH. I don't care.

DANIEL *looks at* CLODAGH.

DANIEL. You don't care?

CLODAGH. No…

DANIEL. So you're conceding?

CLODAGH.… Yes.

THE RECEPTIONIST FKA JESS. You're giving up?

CLODAGH Obviously.

DANIEL. So the money is going to me? I mean Shannon Cross GAA.

CLODAGH. Sure.

DANIEL. Clodagh, what's going on?

DANIEL *goes to touch her shoulder but* CLODAGH *mistakes it as a wrestling move.*

CLODAGH. DON'T! I'm four months pregnant. Don't touch me!

CLODAGH *becomes emotional.*

DANIEL. You're pregnant?

CLODAGH. Yes.

THE RECEPTIONIST FKA JESS. Con… gratulations?

CLODAGH (*blubbing*). Thank you, I'm delighted.

THE RECEPTIONIST FKA JESS. Why are you crying then?

CLODAGH. Because, they're not making me Assistant Vice-President.

DANIEL. I'm sorry, Clodagh.

THE RECEPTIONIST FKA JESS. But Susan said…?

DANIEL. Yes.

CLODAGH. I told Crónán last year that I'd done my time as an executive and I wanted a promotion but not within operations. I wanted organisational. I wanted to be an Assistant Vice-

President. Branch into something else in the firm. He said he'd sort it. He… I've done everything for that man for ten years. Everything. And he won't give me this one thing.

DANIEL. The fucker.

THE RECEPTIONIST FKA JESS. Why didn't he?

CLODAGH. BECAUSE I'M PREGNANT!!!

THE RECEPTIONIST FKA JESS. They can't do that, that's against the law.

CLODAGH. Against the law? Oh thank god for that. The law can stop them.

THE RECEPTIONIST FKA JESS. It –

DANIEL *interrupts* THE RECEPTIONIST FKA JESS, *in an understanding way. He knows the reality of this.*

DANIEL. I'm sorry, Clodagh. Did you tell him or did he guess?

CLODAGH. No, I didn't tell him. And he hardly guessed! I've spent weeks trying to conceal it from him. Making up ludicrous reasons for doctor's appointments, hospital visits and long spells at home with morning sickness. As far as he knows I've donated three whole kidneys in the past four months. I can assure you, he didn't hear this from me but I know who he did hear it from.

THE RECEPTIONIST FKA JESS. And did he tell you 'You're not being promoted because you're pregnant?'

CLODAGH. Of course not it was all: it's just not the right time, I'd like you to shadow with some of the others more before we take that step. You're not ready yet. He asked me to do the professional certificates and I did them. I did them with distinction. You know? But I'm not ready yet. This from the man who can't get himself up in the morning unless I tell him to. He can't even put his own lunchbox in the fridge, for fuck's sake.

THE RECEPTIONIST FKA JESS (*tentatively*). How do you know it's because you're pregnant then?

CLODAGH. Because none of it's true. I've been shadowing *him* for over ten years. Who else could I possibly shadow? And as I left he smiled at me, you know that smile, that wry smile and said: 'Anyway, I'm sure you're going to have enough on your hands.'

THE RECEPTIONIST FKA JESS. Oh.

Pause.

They might give it to you after?

DANIEL. Maybe.

CLODAGH. After what? When the baby's stopped teething or when it's started school? You don't get it. You get to do it all, Daniel. I wanted a baby years ago when my friends were having them. I'd be a young mum, run around after it in the park, have coffees with the girls while our kids play on a swing set. I watched as they all did that without me. Focused on my career to keep going. I had that, that was something I was growing. Something I could develop. Couldn't push it down a slide or dress it in a duck costume babygrow but it was fulfilling in its own way and I probably was dealing with the same amount of bile as you would with a baby, so you win some you lose some. I didn't need to put on a brave face because the girls were doing that for me. You're so strong, I wish I could take it all in my stride like you, it must be very lonely, I didn't start living until I'd had Clive, I can't imagine what it's like having to go to those clinics with all of those tests and injections. But I wasn't going to any clinics and I wasn't going to wait to start living until I'd had a baby and even if I had a baby, I certainly wasn't about to name it Clive. I just gave up. Stopped trying. Helped this company soar, set and exceed all kinds of expectations and it felt amazing. I am the highest paid administrator in this building but I want more. I don't want to help the moneymakers, I want to be a moneymaker. I want to be taken seriously. I was useless in college, went out too much and barely got a degree. Too late to go back and try again because I needed to make a living so I worked and proved my worth. And I was about to be rewarded for that until four months ago. I was five days late and I'm never late for anything. There's a pregnancy test in the back of our cabinet. It's at least three years out of date but I try it on a whim and it's positive. I put it down to it being expired. It can't be right and why am I hoping it's not? I buy another it's positive, it's a two-pack of tests so I try again and that's positive too. I wonder did toilet water splash up and compromise the result? I'm three positive tests deep now and I know I should be jumping for joy but instead I buy three more and check those. Positive, positive, positive. It can't be right. It has to be wrong. This was supposed to be planned, this was not the plan. I was supposed to organise things, arrange them in a way that wouldn't mean everything else would be ruined. But I want it, don't I? Thought I did anyway. Can't take a chance that it would happen again. So I decide it's not going to ruin anything. That I deserve this. I deserve it all. I can have it all. I can keep this from Crónán for a few months. He tells me things are in motion. They announce a new position through internal communications. And I've written the job description. I'm getting the nod from the Vice-Presidents in the hallway. Word seems to have spread everywhere that it's happening. That it's happening to me. A big deal as an administrator. And I'm there strutting around like I've already won it. Until last week something felt different. I couldn't put my finger on it because how could he know? I'd been told with a wink that I would hear by last Friday. And nothing. So when I didn't hear yesterday, I thought fuck it, I deserve an answer. So I charge in there and ask him what's happened? And he tells me that they've decided to give the AVP to someone else. The position I created for myself, that they only know they need because I told them they did and who's it going to? You.

THE RECEPTIONIST FKA JESS. Me?

CLODAGH. No.

DANIEL. Me…? But I didn't –

CLODAGH. Surprise.

DANIEL *is suppressing a smile*.

THE RECEPTIONIST FKA JESS. That's not fair.

CLODAGH. No. It's not. And it's all such a mess and I am so fucking angry and then I feel a heartbeat, pressing up against my stomach. And how can I be angry and resentful at something that is basically the size of an avocado. It doesn't deserve that and I don't deserve this but it's coming and it's happening and I suppose I need to –

A drilling noise is heard. The door pops open.

HR LADY SUSAN *stands there holding a drill with a manic look in her eye.*

HR LADY SUSAN. Lunch hour is over!

HR LADY SUSAN *marches up to* CLODAGH. DANIEL *and* THE RECEPTIONIST FKA JESS *protect her.*

You thought you'd one-up me again, did you? Well I saw you coming this time, didn't I? All locks will be removed from all conference-room doors this week with a new rule of NO food in the conference rooms at ANY time. And anyone found to be in breach of this rule will have to go through me.

DANIEL. And then what?

HR LADY SUSAN. You will be issued a warning.

THE RECEPTIONIST FKA JESS. And if we do it again after that?

HR LADY SUSAN. Another warning.

DANIEL. And after that?

HR LADY SUSAN. There will be a disciplinary hearing.

CLODAGH. For eating our lunch in a boardroom?

HR LADY SUSAN. Yes.

CLODAGH. At a meeting that is only allotted time for at lunchtime?

HR LADY SUSAN. Yes.

CLODAGH. And what if I get a letter from my doctor? Saying I have to eat during lunchtime.

HR LADY SUSAN. You can eat at your desk.

DANIEL. During work hours?

HR LADY SUSAN.... No.

CLODAGH. But what about the meeting?

DANIEL. A lot of holes in this plan, Susan.

HR LADY SUSAN. I'll iron them out. Now if you wouldn't mind leaving this room this instant. Thank you very much.

HR LADY SUSAN looks CLODAGH up and down, realising they're dressed similar.

CLODAGH. We're good here.

HR LADY SUSAN. It is against company policy for employees to eat their lunch in here, Clodagh.

CLODAGH. And what's the company policy on drilling open doors?

HR LADY SUSAN. That's a matter for facilities of which I am the line manager! Now get out!

CLODAGH. No.

HR LADY SUSAN. Clodagh!

CLODAGH. Make me.

HR LADY SUSAN. Now!

CLODAGH. Make me.

HR LADY SUSAN begins to chase them all around the table. She can't catch them.

HR LADY SUSAN. Stop it! Stop it!

They keep running. Changing direction to confuse HR LADY SUSAN.

(*Out of breath.*) That is enough. You know full well, Clodagh, that you shouldn't be doing any precarious activities at this time in particular.

CLODAGH. Precarious activities? And why's that?

HR LADY SUSAN. You know why.

CLODAGH. Are you not going to tell everyone?

HR LADY SUSAN. Why would I do that?

CLODAGH. It didn't stop you before.

The chasing has stopped.

HR LADY SUSAN. Now, isn't that much better? Much more civilised. So off you go, back to work.

(*To* THE RECEPTIONIST FKA JESS.) Julie is starved for her lunch break out there, Jess.

DANIEL. But we haven't voted yet.

HR LADY SUSAN. On what?

THE RECEPTIONIST FKA JESS. On the proposals for the remainder of the CSR budget.

HR LADY SUSAN. Oh so now you're suggesting you were doing something practical after all? Well, I never. Fine. Vote away. And make it quick. I'll tally.

DANIEL. Those in favour of the surplus of the Corporate Social Responsibility committee's budget going to saving the bees say aye.

Beat.

THE RECEPTIONIST FKA JESS *shoots their hand up.*

THE RECEPTIONIST FKA JESS. Aye.

CLODAGH *and* DANIEL *look at each other.*

DANIEL. Aye.

CLODAGH. Aye.

HR LADY SUSAN. The BEES?! Is this some kind of sick joke? How very dare you!!

DANIEL. What?

HR LADY SUSAN (*to* CLODAGH). You know full well that Crónán is allergic to bees! That's why he had electric swatters installed in every room in the building if you don't remember?!

She picks up the electric swatter in a threatening manner.

And how are you going to save the bees then? By denying those in need of swatters? Crónán won't approve of this. Not in a million years!

CLODAGH. He doesn't have to approve of it, he handed the surplus meeting over to me weeks ago. The decision is in our hands.

HR LADY SUSAN. After all he's done for you! To think I was only talking to him a week ago about doing the paperwork for your promotion.

CLODAGH. Really? And you were talking about that how? By showing him my birthing plan?

HR LADY SUSAN. What?

CLODAGH. You told him!

HR LADY SUSAN. Told him what?

CLODAGH. That I'm pregnant!

HR LADY SUSAN. No, I didn't!

CLODAGH. Well you're the only one who knows! You were the only one I disclosed it to so don't act all innocent with me, Susan. You know full well what you did.

HR LADY SUSAN. No I... No I didn't. I didn't tell anyone, I mean I put the information in your file because I am bound to legally. But he doesn't have access to that. Not without my permission. I am the only one with the codes.

CLODAGH, DANIEL *and* THE RECEPTIONIST FKA JESS *look at* HR LADY SUSAN *like 'Sure, Jan.'*

DANIEL. Susan.

HR LADY SUSAN. No, he wouldn't do that. Did he ask you if you were pregnant? Because that's illegal, you know.

CLODAGH (*impersonating Crónán*). 'Anyway, I'm sure you'll have enough on your hands.'

CLODAGH *flashes her eyes between* HR LADY SUSAN*'s face and her stomach.*

HR LADY SUSAN. He didn't…

CLODAGH. He did.

HR LADY SUSAN. That's enough. I am calling him right this second. There are protocols that need to be followed. And he should know that, more than anyone!

HR LADY SUSAN *goes to the spider phone and begins to dial a ridiculously long number.*

THE RECEPTIONIST (*to* CLODAGH). Were they just revenge? The bees?

CLODAGH. In some way, maybe. But two things can be true at once, can't they? Without the bees society collapses pretty quickly really. So whether Crónán likes it or not. He needs the bees.

HR LADY SUSAN (*to the spider phone*). Hello Crónán?

CRÓNÁN (*voice-over*). Sue! How's it going? On my way back to the office. Should be there soon.

HR LADY SUSAN. Crónán, I've just interrupted the CSR committee who were meeting about this quarter's surplus and I'm after hearing some very disturbing information. Can I ask did you meet with Clodagh Rafferty this morning?

CRÓNÁN (*voice-over*). Clods? I did this morning yeah. What's this about a surplus meeting?

CLODAGH. Sorry, Crónán, Clodagh here. The surplus, the ten K left over in the budget. You asked me to sort it a few weeks ago.

CRÓNÁN (*voice-over*). Oh yeah! Sorry. Clodagh! How's it going? Yeah, no, I totally forgot about that. Sure god, I'd forget my head if you didn't screw it on for me. Isn't that right? Anyway, should have told you about that. My bad, soz.

CLODAGH. Told me about what?

CRÓNÁN (*voice-over*). The surplus, I gave it away two weeks back.

DANIEL. You gave it away? Hi Crónán.

CRÓNÁN (*voice-over*). Daniel!

(*Singing.*) 'Daniel is travelling tonight on a train. Lord I love Daniel, I love him so much.'

My man, how goes it? Yeah, see I met an interesting playwright a few weeks ago at a gallery opening. Struggling artist you know yourself. We got talking and I was very taken by her, as an artist of course. Very articulate, really looking to get to grips with the modern world and its challenges.

DANIEL. Okay.

CRÓNÁN (*voice-over*). So I said that my business might have some money that could support her, to write and produce a play as long as it kept within the lines of our business. Not prescriptive per se more inspired by, like the muralist last year. Would that not be a bit boring for you, I said. Not at all, she said. Loads of material and loads of ways to jazz it all up if necessary. Sure isn't all the world a theatre and men and women merely actors on the page.

THE RECEPTIONIST FKA JESS *rolls their eyes*.

Anyway she came back to me a few days later with a pitch of, give me a sec here. There we are now: in the Irish offices of a fund management firm, three employees have the duration of their lunch hour to determine how best to spend the balance of their company's annual Corporate Social Responsibility budget. Behind a locked door and out of sight of management, the task escalates into an increasingly outlandish and hilarious debate revealing secret passions and uncomfortable truths. Great stuff. Sign me up, I said. Not sure how far she'll get production-wise with ten grand mind, but artists seem to survive on worse. They get very creative with it all these days, actors playing multiple parts, doing voice-overs and all of that kind of craic if needs be.

DANIEL, CLODAGH, HR LADY SUSAN *and* THE RECEPTIONIST FKA JESS *all look at each other, suspiciously. Are they in a play?*

Anyway, Daniel, you're the face of the star in the sky. I'll be talking to you. See you later, Clods. Anything else, Sue?

HR LADY SUSAN *afraid to talk, now she thinks she might be in a play.*

HR LADY SUSAN (*quickly*)....No.

CRÓNÁN (*voice-over*). Okay, bye. Sorry again about the mix-up. Sure we're all a bit featherbrained these days, just some of us have better reasons for it than others. Amirite, Clods? Talk to you.

CLODAGH*'s eyes look like they're about to pop out of their sockets.*

A disconnect tone is heard.

They all look.

CLODAGH *goes to switch it off but it won't.*

They all begin to suspiciously walk around the space.

Maybe they realise the wall is a flat.

Maybe someone sees one of the lights.

Maybe another realises that they can't find a door or that they can but it doesn't lead to anywhere.

THE RECEPTIONIST FKA JESS. Are we in a play?

Maybe CLODAGH *realises that she's dressed in a* HR LADY SUSAN *costume and takes it off as if it's infected.*

All four of them look out to the fourth wall and see the audience.

DANIEL. I never agreed to this.

Maybe someone tries to touch an audience member but gets freaked out.

HR LADY SUSAN (*to the audience*). Hi, I'd like to speak to a manager if there's one around. Post-haste.

CLODAGH. You're so embarrassing.

THE RECEPTIONIST FKA JESS. Is this how it's supposed to end?

HR LADY SUSAN (*to the audience*). I said I'd like to speak to a manager please.

THE RECEPTIONIST FKA JESS *continues to wander around the set, fascinated.* DANIEL *equally so.*

CLODAGH *sits down and watches.*

Excuse me –

The lights that HR LADY SUSAN *are under go off. This enrages her.*

She walks to another part of the stage that is still lit.

CLODAGH *picks up a wig and puts it on. Maybe she puts on several items of costume until she looks ridiculous.*

I said, excuse me. I'd like to speak to a manager. This is really uncalled for. Who do I need to speak to about this?

CLODAGH. Honestly, Tiffany. You think they might of let us know we were in a play. I would have had a blowout this morning.

DANIEL *catches on. And begins to put on whatever costume he can find.*

DANIEL. Your mission, soldier, is to capture and disarm the theatre by any means necessary.

CLODAGH. Wait, what? He wants to capture and disarm the theatre? Be my guest / but don't come crying to me when that blows up in your face.

CRÓNÁN (*voice-over*). Thank you for coming to the [*insert theatre name here*]. We hope you enjoyed the show.

The voice-over gets louder like CLODAGH *is being played off during an Oscars speech but he keeps speaking.*

HR LADY SUSAN (*to* CLODAGH). And how is that supposed to help?

DANIEL (*to the audience*). Are you still playing? Are you still playing?

HR LADY SUSAN. I / said EXCUSE ME.

CRÓNÁN (*voice-over*). I SAID thank you for coming to the [*insert theatre name here*]. We hope you enjoyed the show.

DANIEL. Is that Crónán?

CRÓNÁN (*voice-over*). No.

Breath.

Thank you for coming to the [*insert theatre name here*].

THE RECEPTIONIST FKA JESS. Fuck this.

CRÓNÁN (*voice-over*). I SAID THE PLAY IS OVER. GO HOME. NOW. LEAVE. / And... we hope you enjoyed the show.

THE RECEPTIONIST FKA JESS *takes a phone on the table and presses play. Maybe 'Baba O'Riley' by Pete Townshend is playing. This overrides* CRÓNÁN*'s voice-over.*

THE RECEPTIONIST FKA JESS *gets into costume.*

CLODAGH, DANIEL *and* THE RECEPTIONIST FKA JESS *help* HR LADY SUSAN *find a costume and develop a character.*

They all dance and sing as if it's the last song on the dance floor on a Saturday night. While also chasing the lights around the stage as they begin to disappear.

All the lights are gone now. But the music still plays through the speakers. We can feel their bodies move and hear their voices sing.

The music is cut off from the speakers. They sing a cappella in a beautiful harmony.

The song ends.

Blackout.

The End.

www.nickhernbooks.co.uk

@nickhernbooks